PRAISE FOR *SOUL SHIFT*

"As we face more and more demands for our time and attention, it's easy to be distracted from what we value most in our lives. In many ways, we've become disconnected from what gives us joy. With *Soul Shift*, Rachel Macy Stafford has created a hope-filled path to help us rediscover what it means to truly thrive."

ARIANNA HUFFINGTON
founder and CEO, Thrive Global

"Reading this miraculous *Soul Shift* book by Rachel Macy Stafford will plant a loving new voice in your head and cause your heart to mightily expand through the guided processes in the pages. These guided processes will literally lift and reshape your soul."

SARK
succulent wild woman, PlanetSARK.com

"Rachel Macy Stafford is, above all else, a spiritual guide and a compassionate healer. Her books are the kind that take people by the hand, and *Soul Shift* is no different. Indeed, it is a guide for all of us, and if we take Rachel's hand and let her lead the way, we will find transformation on the other side as we enter into her stories and experiences, carefully curated for us to find healing in ourselves and in the world. This book is a safe place to pause, assess, and enter into care for ourselves and one another, making room for the soul shift we so desperately need."

KAITLIN CURTICE
award-winning author of *Native* and *Living Resistance*

"Rachel Macy Stafford is not only an incredible person and gifted storyteller, she is unapologetically honest about things that most people hide. That is what makes her writing so powerful and life-changing. *Soul Shift* is filled with practical takeaways from a self-help perspective, but it doesn't read like one. It's a book that offers guidance without saying where you 'should' be. Read it. And start your journey of self-acceptance and relational healing."

JOSHUA BECKER
author of *Things That Matter*

"In *Soul Shift*, Rachel Macy Stafford shows she is a beautiful balance of inspirational writer and pragmatic teacher. Rachel does not lecture, shame, or claim to know all the answers; she accompanies readers on a unique journey of self-discovery. Page by page, we learn how to reclaim our uninhibited, carefree, curious childhood selves so we can remember what brings us joy, peace, and fulfillment. *Soul Shift* is a trusted guide for weary humans everywhere."

SHEFALI TSABARY, PHD
New York Times bestselling author and clinical psychologist

"Rachel Macy Stafford has the unique ability as a writer to invite you into a safe space that allows you to let down your guard and get curious. Through her combination of vulnerability and timeless wisdom, Rachel writes in a way that provides a respite, a retreat even, from the world. *Soul Shift* is a book you will want to revisit and an experience through which you will find yourself changed—an incredibly rare combination. The best teaching returns us to our own knowing, and *Soul Shift* reminds us of what has always been true. Rachel invites us to survey our lives in the way that only a truly safe person could—with the promise that we're not alone and there's hope for us in the process. Rachel is a guide whose hand you will be grateful to hold, and one who teaches you to lovingly trust and take your own. There is healing in these pages. As a practicing therapist, I'm always looking for books that can be companions for clients doing the brave and hard work of changing their lives. I know I'll be reaching for *Soul Shift* regularly."

MONICA DICRISTINA, MA, LPC
therapist, author, podcast host

"Rachel Macy Stafford understands at her core that the love and patience we give ourselves can transform us from the inside out. Don't just read *Soul Shift*, do *Soul Shift*. And as you do, listen to her words, receive her invitation to embrace courage, and open yourself up to the truths that rest inside of you."

KRYSTLE COBRAN
diversity, equity, and inclusion executive and author of *The Brave Educator*

"Our culture is ripe with the stark messaging that the only way through life is either to toughen up or to lose ourselves in others altogether. But Rachel Macy Stafford invites us to a different path. With profound gentleness, Rachel invites us into the way of deep compassion and fierce kindness for not only others—but also for ourselves. I am thoroughly grateful for the invitation *Soul Shift* provides."

AUNDI KOLBER, MA, LPC
therapist and author of *Try Softer* and *Strong like Water*

"Rachel Macy Stafford never fails to meet me where I am emotionally, offering novel, simple ways to think and feel about big emotions and life changes. Her perspective is a real gift, one I recommend enthusiastically and wholeheartedly."

JESSICA LAHEY
New York Times bestselling author of *The Gift of Failure* and *The Addiction Inoculation*

"This book is a gem. Rachel's focus on taking small, actionable steps to shift how you feel, how you think, and ultimately, the path you choose for yourself, is refreshing and practical, and she guides you along with such genuine warmth."

NATALY KOGAN
author of *The Awesome Human Project*

"Once again, Rachel has created a safe, inviting space for us to be where we are—a place where we can be seen and held with a softness that soothes the soul. Truly. Her honesty and generosity in paying forward what she's learned along the way builds a bridge for us to meet [our] truest selves with the kindness and compassion we are worthy of—which for some of us, myself included, is a new skill. There's a gentleness and ease inside her stories that allow the reader to really feel the shifts. *Soul Shift* offers us a roadmap to reflect and realign with what matters most, with steps that feel empowering."

SAMANTHA ARSENAULT LIVINGSTONE, OLY, MED
Olympic gold medalist, high-performance consultant, mental health advocate

"With the pressure to live in a state of constant distraction, Rachel Macy Stafford's invitation to stop missing our lives is vitally important. *Soul Shift* inspires us to reflect on how we spend our days and recognize the power of presence to help us authentically connect, listen, love, and heal. Read this book now. Thank me later."

JOHN O'LEARY
bestselling author of *On Fire* and *In Awe*

"Life is endlessly shifting beneath our feet. The changes keep coming in waves, unending. The only unchanging thing is Love—our need of it, our desire for it, our capacity to give and receive it. In her newest book, Rachel Macy Stafford helps us make a crucial shift back towards the only thing that truly matters: tending the soul."

CHRISTINA CROOK
award-winning author of *The Joy of Missing Out* and *Good Burdens*

"Rachel Macy Stafford has a way of awakening us to things we need to change in our lives without making us feel guilt for the time we spent getting it wrong. This book propelled me to make real change once and for all. The way she urges us gently but urgently is an art form that only RMS can do! *Soul Shift* is thought-provoking and inspiring, unique and universal. I'm confident everyone who reads this book will begin treating themselves—and the world—with more kindness, compassion, and ease."

MALLORY ERVIN
bestselling author of *Living Fully*

"If you are looking for the book equivalent of comfort food—with a gentle energy boost, a heavy dose of compassion, and zero guilt—*Soul Shift* is it!"

SAMANTHA ETTUS
bestselling author of *The Pie Life*

SOUL SHIFT

ALSO BY RACHEL MACY STAFFORD

Live Love Now:
Relieve the Pressure and
Find Real Connection with Our Kids

Only Love Today:
Reminders to Breathe More,
Stress Less, and Choose Love

Hands Free Life:
9 Habits for Overcoming Distraction,
Living Better, & Loving More

Hands Free Mama:
A Guide to Putting Down the Phone,
Burning the To-Do List, and Letting Go of
Perfection to Grasp What Really Matters!

Rachel Macy Stafford

SOUL
SHIFT

The WEARY HUMAN'S GUIDE to GETTING UNSTUCK & RECLAIMING Your PATH to JOY

sounds true
BOULDER, COLORADO

Sounds True
Boulder, CO 80306

Published 2023

Book design by Meredith Jarret
Illustrations by Kara Fellows

Printed in Canada

BK06469

Library of Congress Cataloging-in-Publication Data
Names: Stafford, Rachel Macy, 1972- author.
Title: Soul shift : the weary human's guide to getting unstuck and
    reclaiming your path to joy / by Rachel Macy Stafford.
Description: Boulder, CO : Sounds True, 2023.
Identifiers: LCCN 2022027681 (print) | LCCN 2022027682 (ebook) | ISBN
    9781683649526 (hardcover) | ISBN 9781683649533 (ebook)
Subjects: LCSH: Peace of mind. | Contentment. | Happiness.
Classification: LCC BF637.P3 S67 2023 (print) | LCC BF637.P3 (ebook) |
    DDC 158.1--dc23/eng/20220629
LC record available at https://lccn.loc.gov/2022027681
LC ebook record available at https://lccn.loc.gov/2022027682

10 9 8 7 6 5 4 3 2 1

To Banjo

Somehow you knew that to become the author I dreamed
of becoming when I was a child I'd need a companion,
but not just any companion—I'd need a cat capable
of doing what no human could ever do:

reveal the worthiness inside me, so it could be reclaimed—

the parts I abandoned,

the parts I lost,

the parts I hid.

Banjo, you are the instrument I needed to become

fully alive,

fully me,

fully free,

and you do it with love and only love.

YOU ARE HERE

Welcome, weary human. I suspect you picked up this book because you are indeed weary—maybe even more than that. Perhaps you are downright fatigued by life. Perhaps you feel misdirected or a little lost, disoriented by the spinning world's relentless demands, endless stream of information, and daily atrocities. Perhaps you long for something to change, a way to escape the pressure so you can simply breathe.

You are not alone . . . in how you feel.

The world feels completely out of control right now, like we are all driving down a crowded highway, bumper to bumper, with construction on both sides; we feel anxious, not knowing how long the traffic will continue, worrying about when we'll get to our destination, and wondering what we should do. As tempting as it sounds to wish for an escape, what we actually need is an *exploration*, one that returns us home to our authentic selves and the joy inside.

Taking the first step to reclaiming your path to joy is not easy, but the fact that you are here with me searching for it is enough to put you on the path to finding it.

You are not alone . . . in what you seek.

You'll be hearing these four words—"you are not alone"—throughout this journey. Yes, this is a *journey*. This is not just a book with pages to flip through and ponder and then eventually forget about. This is a guidebook for you to take with you on a continuous discovery process that will come to life through your introspection, self-compassion, and small, brave steps.

These pages you hold will become your map to joy, presence, purpose, and peace. With my hand in yours, we'll explore eight vital practice areas in the Soul Shift journey:

Presence

True Self-Worth

Letting Go of Perfection

Being Kind to Yourself

Being Your Authentic Self

Self-Forgiveness

Looking After Yourself

Offering Your Gift to the World

If merely reading the names of these practice areas feels overwhelming, let me assure you, this exploration process is not a race, nor does it require you to commit to a fixed itinerary. The eight practice areas in the Soul Shift journey are designed to be explored at your own pace, as many times as you need, in whatever way feels most authentic to you. It is through this flexible, self-paced approach that you'll be able to uncover healing truths and create new, life-giving pathways to a life with limitless possibilities.

Before you begin your Soul Shift journey, it's important to emphasize something:

You are here.

You know the point at which a hiking, biking, or horseback-riding trail begins? It's called the trailhead. There, you can usually find a big map with an overview of the trails and bodies of water you may encounter along the way. On that map, there's a little arrow pointing to a dot that says "YOU ARE HERE."

Let's focus on that dot for a moment.

You are here, and that is significant.

I can only imagine what it took for you to get to this place: You had to carve out time from your daily schedule. You had to make a financial investment. You had to quiet the inner critic, reflect vulnerably on what you might need, and step out of your comfort zone. In other words, you didn't get here by accident. You made both the choice and the commitment to show up in this moment.

You are here, and that is brave.

And this is me, celebrating your arrival and acknowledging the courage it takes to embrace a new journey. If you are anything like me, entering unfamiliar territory can be nerve-racking. You may be wondering: *Is this where I should be? Am I on time? Am I ready?*

Trust me when I say yes, you are at the right place . . . at the perfect time . . . and you've come in the ideal form—just as you are.

Thank you for being willing to traverse a new territory to be here in this moment. If anyone recognizes the significance of leaving one's comfort zone, it is me. I'm a fan of familiarity. I crave consistency. I like having a plan. Knowing what to expect brings me peace. But, as you will read in the pages ahead, opportunities to grow and become who we are meant to be don't typically happen when we cling to what is safe and routine. I'm quite certain I wouldn't be here, writing these words to you, if I'd stuck to familiar terrain. Now, don't get me wrong: it wasn't as if I willingly *chose* to venture out of my comfort zone. Three people were placed in my life to *usher* me out: my husband, Scott, and my two daughters, Natalie and Avery.

Looking back, I had some inclination of what I was getting into when, in 1996, I married a guy who thought nothing of last-minute, out-of-state job transfers in the spirit of "career development." By the time our daughters started school, we'd lived in Indiana, Ohio, Florida, and Alabama. Over and over, I faced the discomfort of establishing roots only to have them ripped up and replanted in new soil.

And if physical displacement didn't present enough challenges, it soon became evident that my daughters' temperaments would also force me into unfamiliar areas. Natalie, with her fierce independence, thirst for knowledge, and zest for adventure, created daily challenges. Avery, with her empathetic soul, big emotions, and snail-like pace, tested me in ways I'd never been tested before. My daughters' inherent natures were vastly different but equally threatening to my desire for predictability. Yet the more I tried to control the natural inclinations of my children, the more pain and discomfort I caused.

I'll never forget telling my sister, Rebecca, in 2010, about the realizations I was having and the changes I knew I needed to make. Rebecca knew I'd dreamed of being a writer since childhood, and I knew she would be a safe confidant.

"I've been writing down these raw and enlightening discoveries," I confided, "and it feels like something significant is happening."

"Rachel," my sister said, her voice low and certain. "You should start a blog! It's basically an online journal where writers share their thoughts and readers can comment, like a conversation. It's becoming hugely popular, and I know several people who could really use your words."

Within days, Rebecca sent me a step-by-step blogging book with a personal note about her belief in me. After extensive research and help from some tech-savvy friends, I started a blog called *Hands Free Mama.* The title encapsulated the pursuit I was on to let go of what *didn't* matter so I could grasp what *did* matter.

A few months into it, I received a speaking request from a woman in my community to talk about my Hands Free journey. My immediate thought was, *Uh . . . what part of "online blog" makes you think I'd want to share this information with a live audience?*

It was hard enough publishing my vulnerable reflections online. To say them out loud and see people's reactions? *No, thank you.* Not to mention I'm directionally challenged, and this woman lived outside the two-mile radius that I usually operated within. (Like I said, my comfort zone was quite small.)

But this person was certain her group needed to hear my story, and her belief echoed a persistent voice inside me that had been saying for a while now, *Just show up and trust that whatever is meant to happen after that will become clear.*

Armed with an old-school printed map and a cutting-edge GPS navigation system, I successfully made the short drive. I was immediately ushered to a room where I was expected to address a group of thirty women I'd never met. As I began to tell my story, my heart raced and my voice quivered, fueling uncertainty that I might not get through it. Scanning the room for feedback, I noticed a woman nodding her head. Sensing she felt a connection to what I was saying gave me the courage to continue. And then, a few minutes later, she wiped away a tear—as if my story was her story and we were in this together.

From that experience, I embraced this freeing truth: **when we see each other's scars, we love each other more.**

When we show up as our most authentic self, we give permission for others to reveal *their* true selves. It is in those vulnerable moments of authentic connection that true belonging is felt.

This was the opposite of what I'd spent my life believing up to that point. I thought I had to hide my insecurities and vulnerabilities in order to be accepted. Yet, in this moment, I couldn't deny the thread of connection I felt with a complete stranger in our moment of shared vulnerability.

My dot to her dot, drawing me toward more authentic connection.

I began to wonder: *If I continue to take brave steps out of my comfort zone, what other dots in my life might connect? And what might the whole picture become if we, as human beings, were to choose to connect our dots bravely, boldly, flawed, and full of hope?*

A LIVING MAP

Shortly after that first speaking event, I began receiving more invitations to talk to adults about living a less distracted life—and to speak to kids, too.

Before my first classroom visit, I dug through an old keepsake box from childhood. I quickly found what I was looking for—the first book I ever wrote. Long before the word *Google* became a verb, my middle-school brain simply liked the silly sound of the word. I decided *Google Island* was the perfect title for a rhyming book about a utopian society where people learn to be kind to each other by being kind to themselves. I'd written the poetic verses for this fun school project and hired my best guy friend, Dave, to sketch the illustrations.

Recovering this book when I had just started writing again after a thirty-year hiatus felt propitious. As I read my innocent, young words, I immediately felt something tugging at my grown-up heart. The message of the story I'd written as a young person still resonated, but with a new perspective that only the adult version of me could comprehend.

I recalled my vision for a world where love, kindness, and acceptance were individually and collectively transformative, but the illustrations by my young friend now felt a bit contrived.

I decided to sit down with a pack of colored pencils and tried to channel my young vision alongside my life experiences. Using broad strokes and detailed shading, I sketched this place I had envisioned in my mind with hues of teal, rose, blue, green, yellow, orange, purple, and red. When I was finished, my inner joy affirmed its correct new physical form. I had reshaped my utopian island to resemble a heart-shaped map, one formed from eight separate but connected areas.

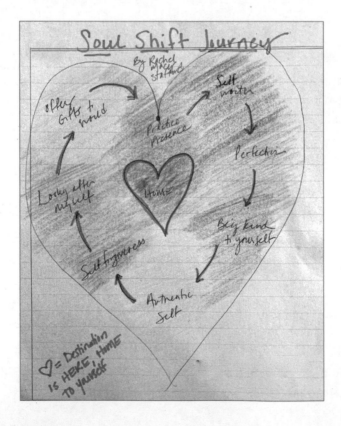

Visually, I was redefining my story in a way that clarified and expanded on the hard lessons I'd learned from the internal struggles I'd faced: that in order to thrive as our most authentic selves, we must first bravely travel through some scary but character-defining territories—presence, worthiness, humanness, kindness, authenticity, forgiveness, self-care, and purpose. Just as our human heart carries oxygen and the vital nutrients we need to thrive to all areas of our body, our mental, emotional, and spiritual journey must have a heart to carry healing energy to and from our soul.

It had taken years of deep introspection and small, brave steps, but at last the vision I'd conjured as a young dreamer had been brought to life. Better yet, this renewed vision wasn't a static utopia meant only for dreams, but rather a dynamic growth process powered by the human heart and capable of transforming lives and communities.

As excited as I was about the way this vision came together, I knew I needed to go beyond simply handing copies of the map to fellow travelers. My calling was to guide willing hearts through these eight areas with one powerful truth to serve as our guiding principle: **when we allow our innermost truths to come to the surface, barriers crumble, the past loses its grip, and we are finally free to create healing pathways on which we can travel as our fully human selves, together.**

This is the essence of Soul Shift, a life-changing journey of uncovering and responding to one's deepest truths in a way that inspires positive change and profound transformation.

And . . . you are here. We will walk this path together.

HOW TO USE THIS GUIDE

As you prepare to embark on the Soul Shift journey, I'd like to offer a few helpful guidelines.

GUIDELINE 1: PERSONALIZE YOUR PATH

You will find the imagery I provided for this journey is that of an idyllic, heart-shaped botanical garden. It is made up of eight distinct areas of exploration that overlap and are connected by stone pathways.

While in each area, you will practice the same small-step discovery process. I refer to these exercises as stepping-stones, and there are four. Their headings in each of the eight areas look like this:

Stepping-Stone One (a Place to Just Be)

Stepping-Stone Two (a Place to Become Aware)

Stepping-Stone Three (a Place to Prepare the Way)

Stepping-Stone Four (a Place to Step Out)

The goal of each practice area is to get to **A Peaceful Spot** (a Place to Let Things Sink In). In that area, you will find three relatable and encouraging stories in which you can immerse yourself and make "notes to ponder."

You'll know you've reached the end of a practice area when you see the section marked "Assurance for Your Pocket." This is a brief word of encouragement to carry with you as you proceed to the next area of exploration.

Although the imagery I envisioned for the Soul Shift journey is that of a garden, yours can be any peaceful place that you feel safe to meander, explore, contemplate, breathe, and grow.

You also may explore the eight areas in any order you wish. Just keep in mind that there is a natural progression from one practice to the next. The tools and insights you gather will eventually form your own living map (located at the back of the book), which you'll use to reclaim the joy you were born to bring to the world.

GUIDELINE 2: REMEMBER YOU ARE NOT ALONE

My teaching approach utilizes personal anecdotes, which include stories about my family, my work, my childhood, my faith. Yet, the essence of this transformative process is not in these personal details; it's in the commonalities we all share: emotion, struggle, growth, connection. While my story's details may look different from yours, the thread that connects us and the work that transforms us is the experience of being human.

GUIDELINE 3: EXPLORE WITH SELF-COMPASSION

After sharing a Soul Shift concept from my own personal experience, I'll invite you to explore your own experiences through writing prompts, sketch noting (visual notetaking), and mind maps. When you encounter discomfort, tenderness, surprise, or challenge during these introspective exercises, please be kind and gentle with yourself. Underneath those uncomfortable feelings is information that will guide and enlighten you on your healing journey, so don't be afraid to feel them.

GUIDELINE 4: VISUALIZE YOUR JOURNEY

And finally, as my story shows, visual illustrations can provide additional context to our feelings and enhance our words. You'll notice each new practice area begins with a title page containing a rock garden marker with a symbol that represents the practice. Use the spacious title page to jot down any insights and observations you make in that area of exploration. The discoveries you make in each section will eventually combine to become part of the bigger picture, your living map. Watch as your Soul Shift journey steadily comes alive, both on paper and in everyday life.

ASSURANCE FOR YOUR POCKET

Beloved companion, it is now time to begin your Soul Shift journey. If you're still holding any doubts about the timing or your preparedness, please unclench your fists and release the weight of doubt using these traveling mercies:

Just because you didn't experience a close, loving relationship doesn't mean you can't cultivate one.

Just because you didn't hear people own their mistakes doesn't mean you can't accept your humanness.

Just because you were loved conditionally doesn't mean you have to keep proving your worth.

Just because you felt misunderstood in life doesn't mean your complexity is too much.

Just because you were denied your feelings doesn't mean it's too late to honor your needs.

Just because you made mistakes doesn't mean you are forever defined by them.

Just because you took an unauthentic path doesn't mean you must stay the course.

You can exit the crowded, high-speed highway and start to trust your internal navigation system. The fact that you are reading this sentence is proof that you've already taken the first steps. *You've already begun to shift.*

The daily responses of love and presence—no matter how seemingly imperfect or small—are creating a better way.

The damaging patterns you're overcoming—not perfectly, but wholeheartedly—are creating a meaningful life.

With awareness and compassion, it's possible to create hope and healing for the present *and* the past, for you *and* for those you love.

Just because transformation seems impossible from where you are right now doesn't mean your weary, brave steps won't turn into a joyous journey of reclamation, in time.

You are here.

I am here.

Together, there is hope.

My hand in yours,

Rachel

AREAS OF EXPLORATION

PRACTICE ONE
PRESENCE

START HERE . . .

I'm starting with love. I'm starting with breath.
I'm starting with stretching my body that carries me despite
the aches.
I'm starting with a hand over my heart.
I'm starting with forgiveness.
I'm starting with a clean slate.
I'm starting with a cup of tea and a crisp new page.
I'm starting with a tearful release.
I'm starting with wind on my face and gratitude on my lips.
I'm starting with my eyes up, not down.
Today, life is calling me to take my own path—
Go at my own pace,
Stop when needed,
Notice the signs, people, and sights meant for me.
Today, life is calling me to show up—
And I take this brave step by declaring . . .
Love is where I'm starting.
May it also be where I am going.
Love IS the way.

E ver since I recovered *Google Island*, the book I wrote as a child, I've been making an intentional effort to connect with that younger version of me, the one I now call "my Dreamer Girl." This was the "me" who knew at a very early age that lovingly responding to myself and those around me brought me joy. Over the past few years, I've spent time remembering what my Dreamer Girl was like.

She couldn't walk by a stray cat without talking to it.

She marveled at the sounds she made with her violin and bow.

She loved the rush of the wind when she swung as high as she could go.

She freely ran through the sprinkler in her bathing suit, unhindered by her squarish body that held an abundance of freckles.

And most of all, my Dreamer Girl's joy was found in filling spiral notebooks with observations, stories, and dreams.

I can't pinpoint exactly when I decided these inclinations were not acceptable and therefore needed to be abandoned. I'm pretty sure it was during adolescence when I began assuming the roles that gained the world's approval—roles like the Planner, the Go-Getter, the Accommodator, the Helper, and the Overachiever—and when accolades took precedence over pleasure.

And those roles were just the beginning. In the twenty or so years that followed, I took on so many roles and expectations that it should have come as no surprise when it all became too heavy to bear.

But it did. I can still see myself at my breaking point—the teacher, the partner, the mother, the daughter, the sister, the volunteer, the completist, the juggler, the people-pleaser, the fixer, all simultaneously coming undone during a morning jog, my well-crafted roles unraveling so quickly I didn't even try to hold myself together.

Fueling my breakdown was a question I got a lot: "How do you do it all?" I'd always taken it as a compliment, but not on this particular day. At thirty-eight years old, I'd reached the very frayed end of myself, and that question loomed before me, forcing me to stop and face the answer I'd been running from.

I could "do it all" because I missed out on life—I missed out on the laughing, the playing, the creating, the connecting, the memory making . . . the living . . . the loving . . . and what I missed I cannot get back.

That truth was so gut-wrenching, I was forced to stop. I collapsed to my knees and I wept for all that I'd lost and the desolate place I was in.

It was then and there that I decided to tell the truth. Looking back now, I realize the significance of that response. For once, I did not push the pain and discomfort away. I allowed myself to feel it, to let truth enlighten me, which is why tears of despair turned into tears of relief.

I'd lost my connection with my Dreamer Girl, the tree climber, the notebook filler, the music maker, the seed planter—but she was not gone. Oh no, she was still with me, in here, hand over heart.

I just needed some time . . . space . . . and permission to reconnect with her.

Dear Soul Shift Companion, does that thought resonate with you? Because here's the reality: as we grow further and further away from childhood, the demands and stress of life increase. We forget we have the power to say yes to what delights our heart and soul, makes us feel alive, and brings us peace. But in order to live an authentic, joyful, and purposeful life, we must remember how to say yes to those very things!

We can do it through the Practice of Presence—an intentional choice to temporarily push away distractions and be fully present in the moments of our life.

Within hours of my emotional morning run, I made this choice for myself.

I was in the middle of making lunches. My younger daughter, Avery, who was almost four years old at the time, was on the sofa watching *The Lion King*. My computer was open, the phone was buzzing, and I was thinking about all the things I needed to do that day. In that moment, I looked up and noticed—really noticed—my child. A clear voice inside me said, "Go be with her. There is nothing more important right now."

Without closing the bag of bread or looking at the clock, I placed the knife across the jar of peanut butter and went to hold my child.

What happened next was something no one had ever done in my whole life: my daughter brought my hand to her lips and gently kissed the inside of my palm, as if offering a silent but powerful acknowledgment of my presence.

This is remarkable, I thought.

Tears filled my eyes.

I was so grateful I did not miss that moment and knew I didn't want to miss any more.

This strong desire to not miss my life is what sparked my Practice of Presence.

Of course, at the time, I did not know it would become my Practice of Presence . . . I called it "going hands free," a term that was inspired by that kiss-on-the-hand moment.

It might sound contradictory to the process, but being a planner, I needed a plan. Realistically, I knew I could not overhaul my life, give up technology, or abandon all my duties and responsibilities, but that initial response I made to heed the inner voice demonstrated it was possible and practical for me to dedicate small increments of time to just being present.

As an experienced teacher of students with behavioral issues and low self-esteem, I knew the impact of small, achievable steps in creating new, positive pathways. Change begins with a behavioral action, and when you change your behavior, your perspective starts to shift, too.

So, I started with ten-minute periods of time during which I set aside my phone, computer, and agenda to be fully present and open to connection.

It was impossible not to notice how one choice produced a ripple of positive outcomes. For example, after opening my pop-up chair at my older daughter's swim meet, I chose not to get out my work in an attempt to maximize the free time. Seeing my open lap and available attention, Avery asked if she could sit there. Holding her made me feel at peace and connected to her. When the meet was delayed, I did not fly off the handle because my plan was derailed. Instead, my daughters and I went and asked the coach how we could help, which he seemed to appreciate.

We got home later than expected that night, but I hadn't yelled or felt that internal pressure . . . which resulted in my falling asleep without the pain of regret. With one choice to be fully present, a series of meaningful experiences were created, lasting far beyond a solitary moment.

As I continued to practice choosing connective presence over productivity, efficiency, distraction, and control, I realized that a feeling of peace consistently came along with that choice; it was as if I was receiving an internal message of encouragement from my soul that said, *This feels in line with how I want to live.*

Now, does this mean that from this point on life was rainbows and butterflies? Absolutely not. The damaging habits and beliefs I'd carried for decades were deeply ingrained, and life continued to deliver unexpected challenges. So, naturally, there were times when I didn't choose a loving, compassionate, or healthy response to conflicts or big feelings. But . . . I was practicing.

And here was the difference: when I encountered a painful external clue—a wounded expression, a troubling comment, an upsetting memory, an uneasy feeling—I did not push it away. The difference was . . . I acknowledged it. I allowed myself to *feel* my response to the discomfort without judgment, so it could be used as information to lead and enlighten me.

Because of this willingness to be present for it all—the remarkable moments and the mundane moments, the peaceful moments and the uncomfortable moments—I was able to move from the painful truth of **I am missing my life** to a new, healing truth:

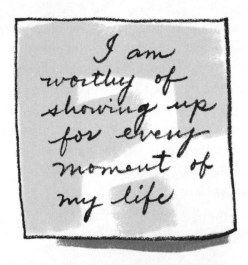

Do you know what this truth did for me? It saved my life. It salvaged my relationships. It reconnected me to my lost Dreamer Girl. It gave me the courage to keep leaving my comfort zone to tell people they are worthy of showing up for every moment of their life, too.

What I have just illustrated, and what you will come to experience firsthand as you navigate your Soul Shift journey, is that in order to move from a painful truth to a new, healing truth, actionable steps must be implemented. I refer to these small steps as "habit shifts." Oftentimes, building awareness is the precursor to the habit shift, which was the case for me in the Practice of Presence.

The awareness process that blazed the trail for my Practice of Presence habit shift was made up of three parts:

1. **Notice** a chance to connect.
2. **Let go** of distraction.
3. **Be** all there.

To help me begin to build the habit of noticing opportunities to meaningfully connect, I designated certain times of day as "hands free," which meant my computer, phone, and to-do list were physically away from me. With every opportunity to be truly present, I became more aware of the damaging impact of our constant accessibility.

Acknowledging that the spinning world was never going to stop demanding my attention, I was motivated to set and maintain protective boundaries around it. Here are the time periods I found most helpful to be "distraction protected" throughout my journey:

- First thing in the morning
- Right before bed
- While making routine drives
- For greetings and departures
- During meals
- During an evening or morning walk or run
- For volunteer or service opportunities
- While caring for pets
- During waiting situations

What made these particular distraction-free increments so powerful and enduring is they became part of our family's daily routine. By repeating them on a regular basis, they became constants my family could count on. Thus, when we encountered disruptive events, like moving, receiving tough medical diagnoses, and losing family members, having these rituals in place meant having a steady foundation for support.

STEPPING-STONE ONE
(A PLACE TO JUST BE)

Dear Soul Shift Companion, I'm sure you have already begun thinking about what times of day would be ideal to keep sacred and protected in your life. It's empowering to realize how one small, intentional act can create such a positive and lasting impact.

Perhaps you're wondering if you should start your Practice of Presence with someone or by yourself. Thinking about this is an important step of preparation. As you read my preparative experience, be thinking about what conditions might be most comfortable for you and most consistently implemented.

I began my ten-minute Practice of Presence with my family members and eventually moved on to practicing alone. At the time, I didn't understand why I needed to go in this order, but now I do.

When I began my journey, being alone with my thoughts was scary and challenging for me. Sitting still and resisting the urge to clean up a mess, make a list, or produce something was also very uncomfortable—I was really good at avoiding feeling. Staying busy and distracted was a coping mechanism for me. Sharing with my family what I was working on offered support and accountability in the event I felt compelled to stray from my path.

After some time of witnessing the impact of the Practice of Presence on my relationships, I felt motivated to connect more internally with myself, especially my Dreamer Girl.

I began starting my day by *not* checking my phone and instead rereading old letters from my grandma. The one thing that always struck me about my grandma was that no matter what mistakes I made, she always saw the good in me. Reading the notes she'd written me throughout my young life felt affirming to my soul. Reading Grandma's letters felt less intimidating than being alone with my thoughts. It was a good first step for me.

I began to spend quite a bit of my distraction-free time periods writing in notebooks, just like I did when I was a girl. Journaling my thoughts, fears, experiences, and dreams opened the speakers of my heart, enlightening me and leading me to the best next step.

What's important to note is that what I did during these distraction-free times, whether I was alone or with someone, whether I was praying, journaling, or simply breathing, really didn't matter. What *did* matter were the conditions: No phone. No computer. No agenda. No to-do lists. No expectations. Just show up with a posture of acceptance and listen to the feelings or thoughts that surface in the stillness.

Making a commitment to touch base with my inner world before touching base with the outer world was enlightening and empowering. I came to realize that listening to the world's opinions and expectations was what often misled me, pulling me away from my true, authentic path.

If we allow it, the world can take hold with a fierce, all-consuming grasp that puts us in the passenger seat. But I've discovered the world does not know what is best for me; my heart does . . . and your heart does, too. That is why it is so important to open our palms each day and receive guidance through the Practice of Presence. Using the chart below, color in the time(s) of day that would be most ideal to keep sacred and protected in your life. Note the expected benefits in the margins.

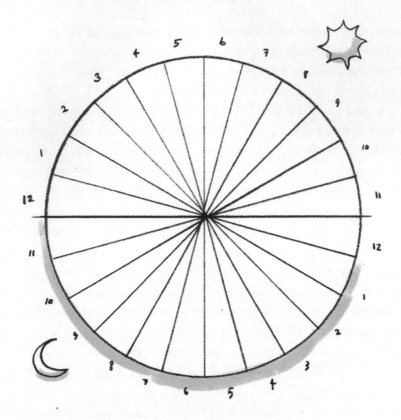

STEPPING-STONE TWO
(A PLACE TO BECOME AWARE)

Dear Soul Shift Companion, prioritizing presence when productivity, efficiency, distraction, and control constantly demand attention certainly isn't easy, but the reward is huge. Until I began living life "off-list," I didn't know the value in opening one's hands and heart to live life as it was happening. Now I know: life's most meaningful experiences never make the list, but that is where the gold is. To determine the most practical and motivating starting point for your Practice of Presence, I invite you to get an accurate reading of where you are right now through self-reflection. Take a few deep breaths and come into this moment. Do not think about what happened earlier today or what's going to happen later today; just be here now and give yourself an opportunity to listen to the guidance of your soul through these check-in questions.

1. What moments of life do you unequivocally not want to miss?

2. What do you think will be your biggest obstacle in creating and maintaining your Practice of Presence? In thinking about the potential obstacles, what are some ways you could overcome them?

Before you read the third question, take a few cleansing breaths. Breathe in for three counts and release for three counts. Please acknowledge what immediately comes to your mind and heart when you read this question:

3. What do you need most right now?

STEPPING-STONE THREE
(A PLACE TO PREPARE THE WAY)

If the last question evoked a strong emotional reaction, or if you drew a complete blank, that is okay. You may reach a place like this more than once in your journey; that's why we call this a practice.

In fact, well into my healing journey, I heard an internal message saying that my constant feeling of overwhelm was not something I could fix alone. When I stopped pushing this voice of caution away, I clearly knew I needed to see a mental-health professional.

During one of the initial sessions with my new therapist, Caroline, she asked me the very question just posed to you: "What do you need right now?" My internal response was a violent scream. I couldn't put the answer into words, but I could see myself pushing back . . . against people, demands, requests, and expectations. This mental image helped me realize that my Practice of Presence had fallen by the wayside, derailing me from my authentic path. As a result, I'd lost touch with my body, my limits, my needs, and my core values.

After that enlightening therapy session, I reinstated my Practice of Presence by stopping by a swing set in my neighborhood playground later that day. While on the swing, I didn't beat myself up for straying from my path; instead, I revisited a list I'd made when I first began my journey. It's a tool I call my "closest" and "furthest" lists, and it helps me recalibrate to my true path of peace whenever I drift or lose my way.

Here's the list I made for myself that day, using this as my sentence starter: "I feel furthest from what truly matters when . . ."

- I am depriving myself of sleep to get things done
- I inhale my meals standing at the kitchen counter
- I critique my appearance
- I judge my success by sales numbers
- I allow the opinions of others to dictate my actions and give up mental space for their criticism
- I feel like my boundaries are not being respected
- I go along with something I don't want to do to please others

But I also had my "closest to what matters" list. On that list I wrote:

- Taking a drive with my daughter, leaving phones at home
- Walking outside in the sunshine
- Talking with a trusted friend who gets me
- Giving my body the nutritious food that it craves and the sleep that it needs
- Playing volleypaw with my cat, Banjo
- Stretching my tight calves until tension eases
- Keeping a folding chair in the back of my car to decompress before heading home from meetings and appointments

Acknowledging the conditions when I feel closest to what truly matters equips me to walk my authentic path and be aligned with the life

I want to live. Equally as valuable is my furthest list, which contains external clues and triggers that indicate a shift is needed.

As I described earlier, my external clue that a shift was needed came from the visceral reaction I had to my therapist's question, "What do you need right now?"

By allowing myself to fully acknowledge my feelings—even the most uncomfortable ones—I realized that amidst launching a book and navigating a chronic pain condition, I'd slipped into old, self-sabotaging behaviors. Revisiting and updating my closest list reminded me that my heart and body are intuitive, pointing out where restorative actions needed to be put into practice.

This connection between mental and emotional intuition began speaking loud and clear, despite the noise of past behaviors trying to drown it out. I became acutely aware of three areas that needed attention right away: Avery was emotionally unwell. It was time to remove a toxic person from my inner circle. And I needed to find out why my soul-renewing meditative walks had become the cause of such unbearable physical pain.

When the podiatrist looked at my MRI, she said, "Rachel, you came just in time. You are very close to having a stress fracture."

When the doctor left the exam room to get the stabilizing boot, I cried with gratitude. If not for a Practice of Presence, I would not have seen the warning signs—not in my foot, not in my child, not in my personal safety. I would have just blown past the red flags until the damage was done.

I was reminded of the debilitating place I was in when I'd started this journey eleven years ago, but this time, I was not back to square one. This time, I had a map that included a place to rest: the Practice of Presence.

It's our beginning.
It's our unburdening.
It's our cleansing breath.
It's our healing hope.
It's our reminder, like a kiss on the hand that never rubs off.
It's our internal compass guiding us to our truest path.

STEPPING-STONE FOUR
(A PLACE TO STEP OUT)

Dear Soul Shift Companion, now that you have readied yourself by thinking about your motivations, ideal conditions, and obstacles, it's time to put this practice into motion. Please make your own personal lists of "closest to what matters" and "furthest from what matters" moments. (Your closest moments could also describe when you feel most safe, free to be yourself, or connected to something larger than yourself.)

Closest   Furthest

Now, look back on what you've written. Would you be willing to make the effort to be in one of your *closest* situations today? If so, please write that effort or action inside the left hand on the following page. And if you find yourself in a *furthest* moment, would you be willing to feel the discomfort it brings and allow it to guide and enlighten you? If the answer is yes, please indicate that in whatever way you'd like in the right hand.

Let's commit to this intention by making a visual reminder. Please grab a sticky note and write down the healing truth we uncovered today. Post it where you can see it often.

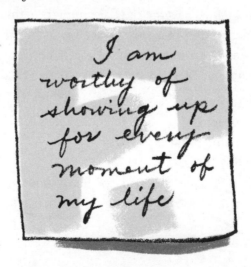

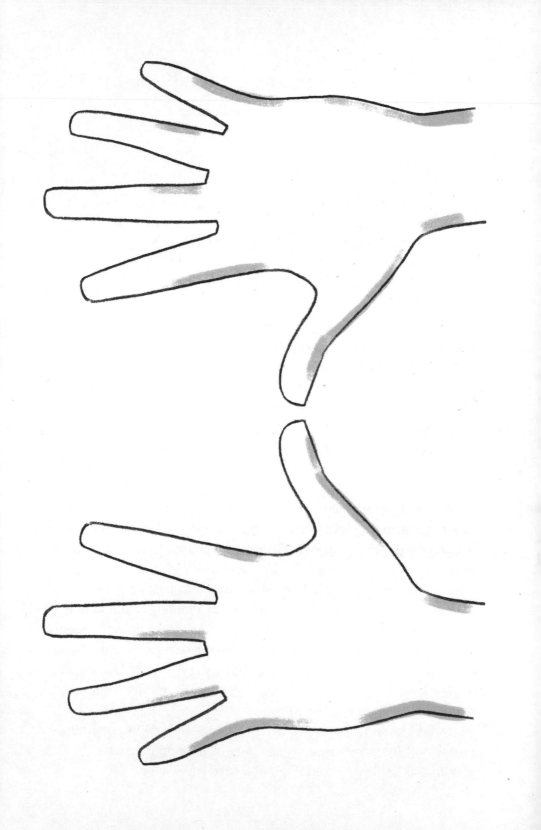

A PEACEFUL SPOT

(a Place to Let Things Sink In)

Stories:

NOTICE YOUR NEEDS

NOTICE YOUR PREPAREDNESS

NOTICE YOUR TENDENCIES

Notice Your Needs

My response to pain and shame is not what it used to be.

I noticed this when I stuffed my size-nine feet into Avery's size-six socks to reconnect with the sentiment that made me purchase them in the first place.

I got them for her right before a time when we would be apart for fourteen days. In sky-blue letters, the toes of the socks read, "I am with you."

As I looked at those comforting words stretched across my feet, I knew putting on the socks was an intentional act, just like the decision I'd made the day before to virtually attend a church I'd always wanted to visit. I'd planned to clean the kitchen while listening to the choir. Instead, I sat down on the kitchen stool, listened, and wept.

It was also an intentional act when I took the folding chair out of the back of my car and set it in a quiet, grassy area after a stressful medical appointment. The sun was shining, and I decided to imagine I was on the beach. I read a few glorious pages in *The Book of Longings* by Sue Monk Kidd and took some cleansing breaths. In thirty minutes, I was in a better place to drive home.

How did I know to act on my own behalf and show up for myself in these ways? By recognizing my feelings of pain and anxiety and responding with this question: *What do I need right now?*

That question became part of my coping toolbox after I'd finally acknowledged that I could really use some help.

To find the help I needed, I Googled my issues of concern with the name of my city. A therapist named Caroline came up in the search. When I read her bio, I felt like she'd written it for me.

At first, it was a little awkward to practice breathing techniques with a stranger through a computer screen. But I soon found the process effectively helped quiet the noise in my head so I could hear my body.

Caroline would then say, "What are you needing right now?"

Without overthinking it, I'd write down the first thing that came to mind.

"You don't have to tell me what you wrote," my helper Caroline would always say, "but you can if you want to."

I always told her, and it felt good to have someone listen, but what felt the best was listening to myself.

We live in a world that pressures women to give more of ourselves than we often have to give. This is revered as being "selfless." But when you break down that term, doesn't it basically imply "less" of our "self"? If our unique gifts are the stamps we are meant to leave on this world, then our "self" needs to be intact and well-cared for. Keeping this in mind when I revisited my need statement each morning, I did not judge myself or feel ashamed for spending time considering my own needs. Instead, I wondered what my unmet need might become as it was fulfilled. That possibility gave me hope . . . strength . . . direction to reframe the narrative.

We have been conditioned to deny our needs, so practicing self-love can feel challenging. I pose this very basic way to start: What if loving ourselves simply means listening to ourselves without judgment or expectation?

What if *self-love* begins with *self-listening*?

"Sounds like you're nervous. You can hold your own hand right now to help you be brave."

"Sounds like you feel tired. Sit down for a moment. You are worthy of rest."

"You feel alone, don't you? Step outside and be held by the birds' songs."

What if loving ourselves simply means noticing our hunger cues, signs of exhaustion, red flags, and internal screams that have been ignored because we have been conditioned to power through pain and discomfort?

I spent much of my life allowing outside opinions to determine what was best for me. But I've decided I will not sabotage myself that way anymore. My body is precious, and it knows what I need if I stop long enough to love it by listening.

Will you join me, Soul Shift Companion? What is your body saying to you right now?

There's no time limit on learning how to love the parts of ourselves we have long abandoned.

Notes to Ponder

I realize I have been conditioned to power through things like . . .

I noticed my need for _____ when . . .

Notice Your Preparedness

They say there are certain things in life you can't prepare for, and mostly I agree with that statement. Yet, I can't help but marvel at the preparedness I felt during an unexpected medical procedure Avery required.

When a pattern of elevated blood pressure readings was detected by her pediatrician, we were referred to a pediatric cardiologist for an electrocardiogram (ECG).

Sensing my daughter's angst as we walked into the red-brick building, I said, "I remember what you told me makes these medical appointments so hard."

The visible relief that registered on Avery's face indicated I was on the right track, despite walking into uncertain territory.

About a month earlier, Avery shared how the biggest source of stress surrounding her ongoing treatment for scoliosis, a harrowing experience that began when she was eleven, wasn't so much the physical pain as much as it was the lack of autonomy. She no longer felt able to govern and protect her own body.

Armed with the specific concerns Avery expressed to me, I knew what questions to ask the medical staff on her behalf:

"May she wear a tank top during the procedure?" (Yes)

"Could she have a female technician?" (Yes)

"Will someone explain to her what's happening?" (Yes)

"Can I hold her hand during the assessment?" (No)

While seated at the foot of the exam table, I noticed the ECG technician struggling to get the electrodes to stick to Avery's skin. The harder the technician pushed, the more labored Avery's breathing became.

Suddenly, I stood up and reached out. As if prepared for this moment, I knew to place my hand on my child's foot. In that instant, my presence became preparedness. I felt Avery relax with the assurance that she wasn't alone and we would get through this test together.

Later that night, I wrote these words:

> I couldn't hold her hand today,
> so I held her foot
> while I held space
> while I held my emotions in check
> to ensure there was room for all of hers.
>
> I couldn't hold her hand today,
> so I held her foot
> while I held her vulnerability
> while I held a posture of support
> to advocate for what she knew she needed to cope.

I couldn't hold her hand today,
so I held her foot
while I held visions of good news
while I held my worries from unraveling
to stay peacefully collected in case she took cues from me.

I am a companion
on a journey I didn't ask for—
no how-to
no instruction manual
no gentle guide to lead us.
I AM the guide,
learning as I go,
but too busy holding pieces of pain and fear to take notes.

Yet, sealed in my brain,
etched on my heart,
is encouragement for my fellow companions,
those keeping close as their beloved navigates a difficult journey.

I step off the path for a moment
to let the sun warm my face and offer a message to my fellow
travelers:

Never underestimate the significance
of that hand on their foot
of that assurance in your voice
of that belief you manage to grasp out of thin air.

Your ability to connect in crisis
without a manual
without a map
is the most direct form of love and comfort you can offer in
times of uncertainty.

Notes to Ponder

The journey I am on that I did not ask for is . . .

I noticed my presence prepared me when . . .

Notice Your Tendencies

"Hey, how are you feeling?" my friend texted.

"Not okay," I typed back.

Initially, my brutally honest response surprised me. Surprise quickly turned to understanding when I thought about what this particular friend said to me after my father-in-law, Ben, unexpectedly passed away. Heather hugged me and said, "You don't have to be strong with me."

Remembering that rare permission, I told her the truth about my current state—although I'm not sure I would've said it quite so directly if my mom hadn't put it into words the previous night.

"It's no wonder you're struggling," my mom said after hearing me describe a trio of stressors I was navigating without my usual and most effective coping mechanism: taking walks.

"I'm worried about you," Mom said several times throughout the call.

Should I be worried? I wondered. *Because I am quite skilled at powering through, putting on a brave face, compartmentalizing the pain and hiding it well.*

Yes, that was true, but there were also new truths:

I was abiding by my podiatrist's medical plan.

I was being kind to my inactive body.

I was celebrating signs of progress, no matter how small.

And I was telling the truth to those I trusted.

That last one might have been the most powerful piece of my healing process. I'd always told myself, "Just smile and keep going," but now I know the necessity of bravely admitting, "I'm hurting."

Acknowledging the pain is the first step toward healing it.

I lived my whole life denying this truth, and it put me on a destructive path, limiting me in some pretty sad ways.

I couldn't be grateful.

I couldn't be creative.

I couldn't be thoughtful or mindful or present, because hiding the unspoken pain inside me took all my focus and energy.

I'm trying to do things differently now. I *am* doing things differently now.

Even though my mom still worries about me (that is just what moms do), I don't. My Dreamer Girl is calling the shots, and she's much more direct and deliberate about our path and what we need. My powering-through days are over; these are now my only rules of the road. Could they be yours, too?

If it hurts, tend to it.

If it brings peace, lean into it.

If it feels scary, ask for help.

If it feels overwhelming, breathe.

If it alternates between good and bad, take it one step at a time.

Notes to Ponder

I noticed my tendency to _____ when . . .

ASSURANCE FOR YOUR POCKET

May the fears blocking your path have less power over you the more lovingly you acknowledge them.

May the uncomfortable feelings you carry get lighter the more gently you sit with them.

May the path ahead look less daunting with this encouraging truth as your homing beacon:

Big, sweeping changes do not create the transformation I seek; transformation and momentum come from taking one small step after another. I am here now, and this is a good place to start.

I can always return to start. I can always return to heart.

PRACTICE TWO
TRUE
SELF-WORTH

START HERE . . .

Typically, I come prepared.
But today, I've got nothing.
So, why even show up? you may wonder.
Because I think it's really important to talk about this—
this idea that we hold no value unless we have something to
offer,
this idea that we must keep producing, no matter what
circumstances we face,
this idea that we certainly can't show up to life empty-handed.
Well, I think the more we show up with nothing,
nothing but our bare souls,
nothing but our skinned knees,
nothing but our hallowed breath,
nothing but our empty hands,
the more likely we are to actually touch something that
matters.
Loving matters.
Connecting matters.
Breathing matters.
Showing up matters.
And if all you've got to give right now is the air expelling from
your lungs,
that's not nothing.
My open hand in yours.

T he Practice of True Self-Worth is one of the most transformative practices I've cultivated on this journey. It has empowered me to make choices by heart, according to my core values and beliefs, rather than by societal standards or the expectations of others.

Did the shift happen overnight? No, not at all. In fact, I am still learning and growing in this area—but a vital catalyst to my self-reclamation process began the moment I recognized I was relying on external measurements and outside approval to determine my worth.

Before I take you back to the moment when I faced the painful truth that sparked my Practice of True Self-Worth, I'd like to define *self-worth* and explain why basing our inherent value on external factors sabotages our chance at long-term joy, fulfillment, and inner peace.

First, a definition: *self-worth* is simply a sense of one's own value as a human being. According to clinical research, self-worth is at the foundation of self-acceptance and self-love. Without a solid sense of worth, it is difficult to feel worthy of love or acceptance from others (Bifulco et al. 2002). This explains why people with a low sense of self-worth tend to believe acceptance is conditional—as if they must act a certain way to receive love. This belief causes people to change who they are depending on their circumstances or the people they're around.

Second, it's important to understand how external measures of self-worth are detrimental to our authentic self. Pressuring ourselves to meet expectations outside of our control detaches us from the core of who we are. It prevents us from hearing our intuitive voice that reveals our deepest, most heartfelt needs. Years can go by before we even realize we've left the most authentic parts of ourselves undiscovered, unnurtured, and unfulfilled.

I experienced this painful disconnect firsthand. I'd like to take you back to a moment in that debilitating period when external factors dictated my life, causing me to see only what I was lacking instead of what I already possessed.

It was New Year's Eve; my husband, Scott, and I were going to take our young daughters to a fancy community celebration. I remember secretly wishing we could stay home, put on our pj's, make popcorn, and watch the ball drop. Instead, I assumed the active social role I'd established in my community; I needed to protect the image I felt was so important to uphold. I remember slipping on my cocktail dress and berating myself for my holiday indulgences that caused it to fit a bit too snugly.

Feeling inadequate, I dismissed Scott when he said I looked beautiful in my black dress. Minutes later, I was curt with my family when they presented me with a beautiful camera to use for my new writing endeavors. I then used the camera to take an unreasonable number of family photos, determined to capture the perfect shot. When I scrolled through the photos, I couldn't help but notice the forced smiles of my daughters, trying so hard to get it right.

The twenty-minute drive to the party was solemn; my family was afraid to say a word that might further upset me.

In the uncomfortable silence, a question surfaced from within me: *Is this how it's going to be, day after day, year after year? This constant feeling of inadequacy . . . of never being enough?*

I turned to look at my daughters, Natalie and Avery, in the back seat. Their sad expressions on what was supposed to be a celebratory night were impossible to deny.

From that uncomfortableness, a painful truth surfaced: **by trying to be someone I am not, I am devaluing myself and hurting my family.**

Later, when I reflected on my behavior that evening, I realized my actions were in direct response to what I was basing my worth on during that time: I was using appearance, achievement, productivity, and approval to determine my worth, yet they did not reflect my core values.

Family, faith, authenticity, communication, creativity, growth, acceptance, kindness, integrity, love—*those* were the things that were important to me.

How had I strayed so far? I wondered, starting to feel ashamed.

But before I got too far down that damaging path, I thought: *Is it any wonder?* Every day, from countless sources, human beings are inundated with messages that tell us we must "be more, do more!" If we aren't vigilant, these misleading messages fuel a subconscious conditioning that we need to behave a certain way in order to measure up, to be worthy.

Becoming aware of this unconscious narrative offered a vital spark to my transformation process. Because I'd started journaling as part of my Practice of Presence, I'd already begun shaping my own definition of success. Page after page held examples revealing how life's most important achievements aren't measured or quantifiable; they are felt in the heart, and they radiate from within.

To illustrate that truth, I attached one of my favorite childhood photos to a page in the journal I was keeping. In the photo, I am leaning against my brick house in Muncie, Indiana. I look confident, happy, and relaxed in a floppy sun hat over my Dorothy Hamill haircut. I'd just completed a two-hour theatrical performance in the backyard with my friend Hillary. I didn't think twice about wearing horizontal stripes and mismatched shorts that day. In fact, there was no long mirror in the house to judge myself against. I just threw on a hat and went outside to play.

As I began unpacking the damaging messages around self-worth, that childhood photo sparked a question: *Why not now?*

My Practice of Presence had revealed to me that small actions—not giant, sweeping changes—create life-changing shifts. I felt emboldened to consider what small step I could take *now* to move toward living more aligned with my true essence.

"HAT DAYS!" my soul responded.

That Saturday morning, I stuck my to-do list in a drawer and bypassed the mirror, which was where self-judgment was the loudest.

I grabbed a ball cap from my closet and walked downstairs to greet my family.

Placing the hat on my head created a mindset of spontaneity, courage, and light-heartedness. In my hat, I was eight-year-old Rachel, the Dreamer Girl who seized every opportunity to laugh, run, play, live, and love, without reservation or restraint.

That day, we got in the car and drove to a playground my daughters had been asking to visit. And from that Saturday on, a freeing two-step process emerged:

1. Throw on a hat.
2. Do what delights your heart.

Most of the time, hat days involved my family and outings in nature. Before long, my new practice started yielding unexpected benefits within my family. One particular experience confirmed the way I wanted to measure my worth for the rest of my life.

It was a paper doll project at Avery's school. The children had been asked to design a character that represented what they wanted to be when they grew up. In a sea of doctors, nurses, teachers, vets, scientists, and professional athletes, there was this odd-looking doll with a helmet on her head.

Thinking I might not understand what I was seeing, the teacher went on to explain, "When Avery grows up, she wants to be a mom—but not just any mom; she wants to be a mom who wears a hat, just like you."

The hats that were reconnecting me with my Dreamer Girl had also made an impression on my daughter. In her eyes, that hat-wearing, joy-grasping woman was someone worth emulating.

While holding that paper doll in my hand, a new, healing truth occurred to me:

I am worthy despite how I might perceive myself

The wording of this empowering truth is important to note. It reveals that I was aware I wasn't suddenly going to deem myself worthy or enough. To make this shift from external to internal measures of worthiness, I needed to be honest with myself. Aligning my worthiness with the yearning of my heart, rather than societal standards, was not going to happen overnight, but taking small steps to show up even when I felt inadequate or unprepared would forge a path to much deeper, more lasting change.

Looking back now, I realize the significance of the hat. Not only did it serve as a tangible anchor to the core of who I am, but it also served as a boundary setting tool. Hat days meant no mirror, no overworking, no text responses. Placing boundaries around what I would and would not do protected my time, focus, and energy for relational and emotional investments that mattered to me. Setting this boundary was a big step. As someone who derived her worth by pleasing and accommodating, boundary setting did *not* come easy. Through education and introspection I've come to understand why.

Boundaries are an expression of self-worth. They communicate to other people who we are, what we think, how we feel, and what we will and will not tolerate. If you are like me and were taught that in order to feel safe, loved, or accepted you needed to be overly accommodating, expressing your true feelings feels risky because you're exposing yourself to rejection. But expressing one's true feelings means living aligned with our own true essence, which is empowering, healing, and revitalizing.

Here's the good news: no matter how you lived or what you believed up to this point, it's not too late to begin honoring the parts of yourself that have been silenced, denied, or neglected.

STEPPING-STONE ONE
(A PLACE TO JUST BE)

Dear Soul Shift Companion, in order to prepare for a Practice of True Self-Worth, it's important to consider what areas of your life could benefit from better boundaries and how they are impacted by the ways you measure your self-worth.

The following boundary assessment tool can help you do this. Its purpose is to help you identify instances when your needs or limits are being violated or your values or desires are being dismissed. As you read each statement, I encourage you to go beyond "yes" or "no" and really give yourself permission to expand on why or how.

Please remember: you are in shame-free territory. Resist the urge to place judgment on any of your responses. There are no "right" or "wrong," "bad" or "good" answers here. You are simply gaining valuable awareness by being honest with yourself. Treat uncomfortable feelings as guidance. Through this courageous, introspective process, you are building a foundation for creating and maintaining healthy shifts in your life.

BOUNDARY ASSESSMENT TOOL

- Can you recall a time when you were treated badly and failed to speak up?
- Would it be accurate to say you give away too much of your time?
- Are there moments when you agree with people when you actually feel like disagreeing?

- Are there times when you say "yes" when you just want to say "no"?
- Have there been moments when you felt guilty after taking some time to honor your needs?
- Do you often feel taken for granted by others?
- Would you define any of your relationships as unbalanced, meaning you're always giving and the other person is always taking?
- Are there times when you feel responsible for other people's unhappiness, like you're supposed to fix it?
- Are there times when you are what other people want you to be and not who *you* want to be?
- Would it feel accurate to say you have a chronic fear about what other people think of you?

At some point in my life, I've said "yes" to every one of these statements, which is what eventually provided the awareness I needed to create this enlightening tool. Now, whenever I find myself feeling resentful or agitated, I am able to recognize those feelings as indicators that my boundaries are being violated. I find the appropriate statement on the assessment list and go beyond the "yes" response to gain information, like this:

> "Yes, I feel taken for granted when that person only reaches out to me when she needs something for her business endeavors. I feel angry I have allowed myself to be used and devalued by this person. What I am going to do differently now is _____."

Expanding on the resentment statement from the assessment tool is what prepared me to start setting healthy boundaries around this person. I encourage you to give it a try. The next time you feel resentful or frustrated, ask yourself, "Is my anger trying to tell me something? Are my boundaries being violated?"

As you face these situations, you might feel your pulse racing, your shoulders clenching, or your hands getting sweaty. You might think,

This is really hard and uncomfortable. You are getting in touch with your authentic self—your needs, limits, preferences, and desires—which is difficult but vital preparation for honoring yourself.

STEPPING-STONE TWO
(A PLACE TO BECOME AWARE)

Dear Soul Shift Companion, overcoming the tendency to base your worth on external measures and begin living in alignment with your true essence is a transformative process that occurs over time, but you must have a starting point. Changing an undesirable situation begins with an accurate assessment of the current situation, and that is what the following check-in questions are designed to help you do. As you reflect on the prompts, please push away distractions, judgment, and preconceived notions of how this exercise is going to turn out. Let yourself be here right now, in your body, and feel what you feel. It is through this increased level of awareness that you will be able find the most accessible path for you to begin honoring yourself.

1. How do you measure your self-worth? When I mentioned external measurements like appearance, achievement, and approval, did any of those resonate? Are these measurements in line with your core values?

2. Do you change who you are in certain situations or around certain people?

   If the answer is yes, I want you to explore that a little bit. How do you change when you are in the presence of a certain person? How do you adapt or conform when you're in a certain situation? How does that feel?

3. Do you feel in tune with your intuitive voice or inner knowing?

If the answer is yes, how have you let your intuitive voice guide you recently? If the answer is no, what do you think interferes with your ability to hear or trust your intuitive voice?

STEPPING-STONE THREE (A PLACE TO PREPARE THE WAY)

No matter what you wrote in the spaces above, no matter your situation or past reputation, you can start forging a path to acknowledge your worthiness today. Your shift from seeking external validation to nurturing inner transformation happens through a Practice of True Self-Worth, which starts with honoring all of your feelings.

Honoring my true feelings was challenging at first; it helped to have a trusted friend in whom I could confide. Some of the most profound shifts in the area of self-worth have come from being vulnerable and honest with my friend Shannon. I can vividly recall a specific conversation that was especially eye-opening.

About five years into my writing career, I confided in Shannon that being an author was no longer bringing me joy. I told her that as my platform grew, so did the number of duties, expectations, demands, favors, and requests I received. I admitted that I commonly felt stressed, depleted, and used.

"I just want to write messages that help people feel seen and less alone in their struggles—but so much else is expected of me, and those other things are contaminating my joy and purpose."

That is when Shannon said these unforgettable words: "Rachel, you're a mapmaker, not a baggage carrier, not a tour operator, and not a travel agent. You are there to guide and accompany people through their own journey; you are not responsible for carrying stuff that does not belong to you."

I can't emphasize enough how powerful this imagery was for me and how often I revisit it. Recently, I used Shannon's analogy to gain clarity on the roles I want to serve in my life.

I made a list with two columns: "What I love about my job" and "What I dislike about my job." From the list, I classified my occupational tasks and expectations into roles.

The list made it abundantly clear that I was spending too much energy fulfilling aspects of the job that were either 1) assigned to me or assumed of me, or 2) purposeful at one point in time but only hindering me now. And continuing to fulfill these roles was not only counterproductive to my goals but also harmful to my well-being.

While some of the depleting roles could be removed completely, others were nonnegotiable. Most importantly, the act of naming these depleting roles created the awareness I needed to make better choices with my time, focus, and energy. I was then able to identify five self-appointed roles that fulfill me and serve the world.

I am a connector, not an influencer.

I am a guide, not a guru with all the answers.

I am an encourager, not an advice giver or problem fixer.

I am a soul-builder, not a social media strategist.

I am a mapmaker, and I am on a lifelong journey to grasp the moments that matter.

When I shared this epiphany with my online community and retreat participants, the response was incredible. Many of them publicly declared what they are and what they are not. Here are a few examples . . .

I am not a peacemaker. I am a bridge builder.

I am not superwoman. I am human.

I am not an outlet to plug into. I am a candle to share my light.

I am not a victim. I am a survivor.

I am not a doormat to walk on. I am a companion to walk with.

I am not a planner. I am an experience giver.

I am not an overcompensator. I am a partner.

Dear Soul Shift Companion, does this exercise inspire any declarations of your own? Are there roles you're fulfilling that may actually be hindering you, or even harming you? If so, please sit with that for a minute. Give yourself this time to think about who you are and who you aren't, or maybe what you were and what you don't want to be anymore. To help, I have provided a reflection prompt to inspire you to consider what roles in your life are no longer serving you and may be blocking you from a path where you can thrive.

Role Reflection

Can you think of any roles you currently fulfill that you never asked for? These could be roles you've been assigned just because people assume you'll do them, roles you went along with to avoid rejection, or roles you adopted in the past as an act of self-preservation.

Based on your responses above, design a Reclamation Desk Plate using these prompts:

I am not a _____ ; I am a _____ .
This is how I want to show up in the world.

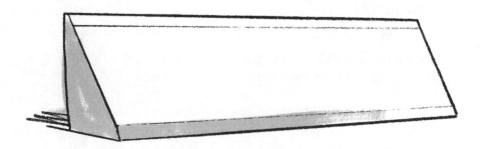

This relationship between roles, self-worth, and boundaries has intrigued and inspired me so much over the past year. My friend Kerry and I routinely talk about the progress we are making in this area. During one such conversation, Kerry described a groundbreaking moment of awareness. She has graciously given me permission to share.

Kerry's role in her dysfunctional family of origin was to take care of everyone at the drop of a hat. In her forties Kerry realized she had assumed the role of caretaker in most of her relationships. Continuing this role in adulthood and carrying it over into other relationships was causing self-betrayal, lack of boundaries, exhaustion, guilt, and pain.

With this awareness, Kerry knew it was time to release herself from this role. During a series of meditative sessions with her internal caretaker/peacemaker, she was able to say, "You served me well, but I don't need you anymore. You can go now."

I think of this powerful role release example whenever my recovering People-Pleaser steps in. I gently say to myself, "I know you are trying to protect me from being rejected by this person, but I am choosing not to reject myself instead."

My friend Diane tells me that she has begun saying to her recovering Conformist, "I don't have to go along. I have the power to do what is best for me."

In these examples of releasing roles that no longer serve us, we gain opportunities to invest in new, meaningful roles. So, rather than spending your precious time and energy in the land of resentment, depletion, or bitterness, you can begin thriving in the areas of self-worth and inner peace.

STEPPING-STONE FOUR
(A PLACE TO STEP OUT)

Dear Soul Shift Companion, it is now time to begin your Practice of True Self-Worth. In essence, this practice addresses one of the biggest obstacles to living a fulfilling life: how do we get from identifying the roles in which we wish to invest our time and energy to actually living them out?

The answer: by honoring ourselves.

Setting boundaries, one small, self-honoring act at a time, serves as the bridge from *external* to *internal* measures of worthiness. To help you gain momentum on your path toward meaningful measures of worth,

I've broken down my ongoing self-reclamation process into six steps. As you read through them, notice which step speaks to you the loudest.

Step 1: Acknowledge the Origin

Each of our lives is a unique recipe of our own experiences, so our coping mechanisms for negative feelings can be just as complex. It's important to try to isolate and define your specific triggers.

Here's one example. If you grew up feeling like you were unable to establish personal space or lacked control over your life, you may have learned to seek external approval instead of trusting yourself. Furthermore, you may have associated being overly accommodating with feeling safe, loved, or accepted. As an adult, you now realize that trying to meet expectations outside your control (other people's approval or opinions) detaches you from the core of who you are, and you are not willing to do that anymore.

Step 2: Celebrate Your Awareness

You are now aware that pleasing is *not* the path to love and acceptance. The notion that worth must be earned is not your truth, and each time you deny your needs in order to "keep the peace," you are severing the connection to peace within yourself.

This understanding is fuel for your self-reclamation journey. Celebrating this newfound awareness, time and time again, cannot be underestimated.

Step 3: Pause

Now that you are aware, you can pause anytime you feel compelled to go along with something even if it's not what you want to do. Pause and remind yourself, "I have a choice." You do not have to go along just because someone wants you to. Ask yourself, *What do I want to do?* And then take a deep breath and say it.

Step 4: Practice

Voicing your needs takes awareness, courage, and practice. If you fail to speak up and realize afterward that you went along when you didn't want to, gently remind yourself that this was how you navigated life for a long time. Change doesn't happen overnight, but **you are trying**. Choice by choice, you are listening to your needs and voicing them. This is significant.

Step 5: Notice

Notice what happens when you voice your needs. You may be surprised to get a positive response. If you *are* rejected, remind yourself that you are not responsible for other people's reactions to your boundaries. Although the external pushback may feel uncomfortable at times, you will come to cherish this newfound sense of internal peace, a priceless benefit of self-reclamation. The more you practice self-valuing behaviors, the less power other people's opinions will have over you.

Step 6: Learn

As you begin to really listen to yourself, you may find unexpected surprises. Give yourself permission to be curious about your true likes, dislikes, interests, and inclinations. Coming to know yourself will help guide you toward the boundaries you need to live as your most authentic and cared-for self.

Dear Soul Shift Companion, which of the six steps most resonated with you? Go back and read it out loud. Keep in mind that you will have countless opportunities to use this step in the days and weeks ahead. These are actually opportunities to create harmony *within yourself* by expressing what you will and will not accept for your life. Harmony within yourself ripples out, creating harmony in your family and in the world. What an important impact you are making! Please honor this commitment to create more harmony by writing down the self-honoring action you plan to take this week:

When you use it, document it on your map and celebrate! Choice by choice, listening to your needs and voicing them is how you'll move from merely surviving to gloriously thriving.

Please grab a sticky note and write down the healing truth that we uncovered today. Post this reminder where you can see it often:

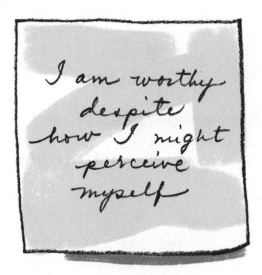

A PEACEFUL SPOT

(a Place to Let Things Sink In)

Stories:

HONOR YOUR RED FLAGS

HONOR YOUR ABILITY TO CHOOSE

HONOR YOUR RIGHT TO FLOURISH

Honor Your Red Flags

I've gotten more comfortable with setting boundaries, particularly when it comes to rejecting the roles people automatically assume of me.

What still feels very uncomfortable is the fallout. Perhaps you know from personal experience that when you stop fulfilling people's expectations of you, they're often not happy about it.

This person was not happy about it.

I was okay with that.

But as time went on, I worried. Fear of disappointing and/or hurting this person began to creep up. The recovering People-Pleaser in me considered reaching out to make sure the person was okay.

But before I did, I played out that scenario in my head. And when I did, a giant red flag went up, and eight profound words came to mind: "Don't throw good energy at a bad situation," my sister, Rebecca, once said to me.

She went on to explain that we are "completists," meaning we have the tendency to try and resolve *all the things*, even things people put on us that we did not want or ask for—which eventually depletes us, frustrates us, and causes us to abandon ourselves.

"Don't follow up. Just let it go," my sister advised.

That advice was exactly what I needed then and what I needed now as I fought the urge to be a completist and my fear of being perceived as a bad friend. By extending compassion to myself, I was able to hear the voice of my self-protector indicating that the best choice for me was to NOT follow up with this person.

Deriving my self-worth from approval, achievement, and productivity is something I did for a long time. I am getting stronger at deciding what I will not tolerate and refusing to take responsibility for the way people respond to my decisions.

This is hard work, and I won't always make the self-honoring choice, but I'm making progress using my sister's advice along with these discerning questions:

Do I really want to keep this conversation going?

Do I really want to open this can of worms?

Do I really want to deal with this toxicity anymore?

Do I really want to spend more energy on this?

No? Well, then don't throw one more ounce of energy at it.

I haven't always believed it, but now that I know, I want to tell everyone who will listen: We have a right to keep toxic elements off our property, out of our minds, and away from our hearts. Would you like to start protecting yourself, too?

It's not too late to listen to our inner protector who knows when it's time to draw the line.

Notes to Ponder

I honored a red flag when . . .

Honor Your Ability to Choose

My current favorite picture of my sister and me is a candid shot on the front porch of her North Carolina home. We are laughing hysterically, which makes us look more like mischievous kids than middle-aged adults. It's nighttime, and we are bundled up with winter hats and warm coats.

I'd driven several hours to get to her house after leading a retreat. I knew I would need this reprieve, so I told Rebecca I was coming. I'm not really comfortable with saying what I need. It's kind of a new thing for me. For decades, I believed it was "easier" to just go along with things, even if it wasn't what I needed, wanted, or was in my best interest.

But a pattern of self-sabotaging behavior pretty much comes to a halt when a crisis occurs.

On our best days, we might spend countless moments overthinking our decisions, worrying about the outcomes and wondering how everyone around us might react. But when we are faced with a crisis, much like a doctor in the ER, there's no time or energy for the nonessential; the only priority is to triage what is happening right in front of us, trusting our instincts and expertise. The only relevant question is: What do we need to triage, to repair, to heal right now?

> I know I need to surround myself with people who
> Don't judge me
> Don't hand me $2 clichés
> People who
> Allow me to change
> Allow me to grieve
> Allow me to grow
> People who slow down when I tell them I can't walk that fast anymore
> People who give me time to find my words or just sit with me in my silence
> I'm not who I was before

And just when I thought my ability to laugh was damaged beyond repair, I heard it—

Joy . . . silliness . . . ease, bubbling up from my chest, the same chest that hadn't fully exhaled in six months due to a family crisis.

But this night, this night at my sister's house where I said, "Becca, let's just bundle up and dine by the firepit . . ."

I exhaled.

I'd told my sister what I needed.

And she said something like, "My home is your home, Rach."

She said it with such love that I nearly cried.

But instead, I laughed.

And it was a glorious sound.

You know what created the space for it? A glorious thing called BOUNDARIES.

If you're like me, boundaries are hard to set, but they are lifegiving AND lifesaving. **Boundaries are the greatest act of self-care that exists on earth.** Not only do they keep out what you don't want in your life, but they also create space for what you *do* want.

No matter how long you've neglected your needs, your desires, your dreams, it's not too late to start acting in self-honoring ways. Would you like a starting point?

Dear Soul Shift Companion, the next time you're in a situation that requires your opinion or participation, ask yourself: *What do I want to do?*

You'll probably have a sense of what other people want to do . . . and I bet you'll have a sense of what other people want YOU to do . . . but the question is: What do YOU want to do?

It might be hard to answer at first—after all, we've been conditioned to run things through the Filter of Approval. But let's remember: we have a choice.

What do *you* want to do? What do you *not* want to do?

First, respond to yourself, and then say it out loud.

Not everyone is going to honor your words. Some may even tell you why your expressed need is wrong.

But that's on them, not you.

I'm learning this, and it hurts to see some people choose not to stick around, to deny what I say I need in order to heal and thrive as my most authentic self.

That's okay.

I am finding their departure is not the end of the world—more like the start of something glorious and long overdue.

Notes to Ponder

I honored my ability to choose when . . .

Honor Your Right to Flourish

SPEAKING OF REJECTION (PART I)

Loyalty
True-heartedness
Trustworthiness
Dependability—
I pride myself on these things.
This is who I am.
I don't give up on people.
I forgive easily.
I see the best, even if I have to dig deep.
But there comes a point
when your ill treatment
your disinterest
your un-prioritizing
of me
has pained me for the last time.

I will no longer try to save what's dying.
I'm walking away.
"I can hold my own hand and be brave," my daughter once
told me.
I remember now.

I will not expend any more energy to stay connected to what
depletes me.
I will no longer nurture a one-sided relationship.
I will no longer be the recipient of others' leftover scraps.

Out there is a heart in dire need of friendship—
a person who would relish
my kindness
my time
my laughter
my love
all the best parts of me you so carelessly discount.

Only I decide how many chances to give
and I've decided
enough.

I'm loyal—to a fault, some might say
but it is not a fault—it is a gift.

And I choose to give my loyalty
to someone else.

I'll begin with me.

SPEAKING OF REJECTION (PART II)

Just because you haven't found your people,
doesn't mean your ability to connect has been lost.
Just because local circles haven't opened for you,
doesn't mean your ability to belong is broken.

Just because nobody around you "gets" you,
doesn't mean you are too complex for understanding.

Just because no one in your vicinity shares your interests or
passions,
doesn't mean you are uninteresting, or your passions
are unworthy of pursuit.

Your people may not be within walking distance, but believe they exist.

Your community may not be easy to find, but believe it exists.

Rejection and isolation can take damaging tolls, even lead you to believe there is something "wrong" with you. But have you considered this?

Maybe it's not you . . .
Maybe it's where you've been planted.

Perhaps the soil, sunlight, and conditions in which you are trying to live, breathe, and flourish are what's wrong *for* you.

Uprooting yourself from a depleting environment, even briefly, is significant. Yes, it requires effort, courage, creativity, and patience, but you are far too valuable to remain in a place where you cannot thrive.

Maybe it's not you . . .
Maybe it's where you've been planted.

Your precious self is worthy of good soil.

Notes to Ponder

I honored my right to flourish when . . .

ASSURANCE FOR YOUR POCKET

May someone's disapproving words, "You've changed," not deter you.

May someone's dismissal not drag you down.

May you continue onward using this protective truth as a soothing salve:

Consistently rejecting my inherent self creates a wound far deeper, far more painful than the external rejection I received today.

I won't always make self-honoring choices, but I am trying. Healing work like this takes time—and for the first time in a long while, I know I'm worthy of taking as much time as I need.

PRACTICE THREE
LETTING GO OF PERFECTION

You can be a good parent and still have struggles with
your kids.
You can be a good employee and still have less-than-
stellar results.
You can be a good friend and still find friendships hard
to navigate.
You can be a good partner and still get weary from the effort.
You can be a good human and still have parts of yourself you
want to hide.
You can be a good caregiver and still feel resentful.
You can be a good role model and still make mistakes.
You can be a good adult child and still wish things had been
different growing up.
You can be a good helper and still hope someone remembers
your needs.
You can be good *and* still.
Please remember this as you take brave steps away from the
territory of Not Enough.

Remember:
You are human.
You are trying.
You show up.
You love.
You love.
You love.
Without fail, you love.

You can be good and still . . .
be human.

Now breathe and proceed . . .
with love.

hope you're feeling more and more secure with each new, small step in this journey we're on together. I say "together" because, as I learned from my friend Shannon, my role in life is not to be an expert telling others how to live, but to be a guide showing others the path I've explored. As you've probably noticed in the previous territories, I share a lot of details about my own life. That is because I believe the most helpful guides are the ones who reach out their hand and say, "Here, let's look, together, at how change happens in the real world."

Ultimately, this journey is about *your* transformation. The discovery process on the Soul Shift journey is limitless, ongoing, and personal to *you*. No matter what did or didn't happen yesterday, today offers an opportunity to gain new insight that will take you one step further in your journey of self-reclamation.

Each time I guide someone through a new practice, I feel a sense of hope and excitement. It doesn't matter if it's my second or twenty-second time exploring a Soul Shift territory with someone, I know there's enlightenment waiting ahead if we're willing to keep an open heart and mind. This promise especially holds true for a Practice in Letting Go of Perfection.

A common remark I hear from people when embarking on this practice is, "That's not me. I don't try to make things perfect."

If the word *perfection* in the title of this practice is throwing you off, I'd like to offer a helpful distinction. This terrain isn't as much about overcoming the *need to be perfect* as it is about overcoming the *fear of not being enough*.

My fear of inadequacy in areas like appearance, productivity, and status drove me to unhealthy places for many years. I wanted the outside world to view me as a happy, vibrant, successful person who juggled all the balls life tossed at me with ease. I actually did a pretty good job at keeping up that facade . . . well, as long as everything went according to my plan. When something *didn't* go as planned or threatened to derail my schedule, I'd overreact. It got to the point where exasperated sighs, eye rolls, and complaints were my default response. In my world, minor inconveniences were viewed as major catastrophes. This is what happens when you base your happiness on specific outcomes, many of which you have little or no control over.

Living in a perfection-seeking state creates tunnel vision. You become so focused on what is wrong that you fail to see what is right . . . good . . . holy . . . and true. Before you know it, your joy is gone, and you rarely feel content with your life or those with whom you share it.

This painful truth was revealed to me through four words Scott said to me as we were about to leave for a family vacation. I was upset over various things—the dishwasher acting up, the late start getting on the road, and a few other minor hiccups I can't even remember now. What I *do* remember is the moment Scott suddenly stopped backing out the car, turned to me, and said in a somber tone, "You're never happy anymore."

Although I wanted to scoff and say, "What are you talking about?" I couldn't, because . . . he was right.

Now, like a good perfectionist, I refused to come out and say, "You're right," but I didn't deny or dismiss Scott's statement either. I accepted what he was saying because my soul recognized it as truth.

When I think back to the moment that sparked my Practice in Letting Go of Perfection, I ask myself, *Why did Scott's observation get through to me?* He'd pointed out the hurtful impact of my controlling ways before. Why did I accept this statement at this particular point in time?

I think it was not so much *what* Scott said as it was *how* he said it. It wasn't spoken as a criticism or judgment of me—it was spoken as a grave concern, a deep grief, as if someone Scott loved very much had gone away.

I remember turning to the back seat of the car to see if my daughters had heard their dad's words. I worried that my greatest fear would be exposed—that I did not have it together the way other women in my community appeared to. Even though I'd gone to unhealthy lengths to make myself appear as the person I thought I wanted to be, behind the facade was someone I did not want to be . . .

I didn't want to be someone who:

- Ruined perfectly good days by putting excessive pressure on myself or the ones I love

- Caused my family to feel like they were a constant disappointment
- Let expectations, plans, and appearances take priority over relationships, laughter, and memory-making
- Couldn't apologize or laugh at myself
- Was perpetually exasperated over minor mishaps

I didn't want to stand on the outskirts of every moment and experience every milestone as a critical observer rather than a joyful participant.

And that was when I faced a painful truth: **I am sacrificing my joy and peace to uphold a facade of perfection.**

It was in that moment that I admitted I was living in a state of perpetual disappointment. My happiness was conditional, based on requirements of tasks being completed, notes being in pitch, plans running accordingly, and hairs being just so; I was setting myself up for misery.

Not knowing if or how I could ever find my way to a more joyful state of being, I prayed for the courage to take one small step out from behind the facade.

A few weeks after making that prayer, I took the first step.

My daughters and I were exiting our neighborhood on the way to school. In typical taskmaster fashion, I'd corralled everyone to the car. When I noticed the spring morning was particularly pleasant, I rolled down my window.

That's when a little voice inside encouraged me to look up. Normally, I would have ignored this internal nudge, but in light of my earlier prayer, I responded differently. I gently took my foot off the gas pedal and peered through my windshield. As far as my eyes could see, the sky was filled with a million little white clouds, as if the stuffing inside a giant pillow had been joyfully dispersed.

When I felt a strong urge to pull over, I didn't resist. My brain warned me that stopping might make us late to school, but I followed my heart anyway.

With the car pulled safely off to the side of the road, I slid open the shade covering the sunroof above my daughters' heads and said, "Look!"

They both gasped in astonishment. When I went to take a picture of the blanketed sky, it was my turn to gasp. There, on the glass of the sunroof, was the most distinct little handprint.

Natalie spotted it too; knowing I liked things clean and tidy, she asked if I wanted her to wipe it off.

I shook my head no, suddenly overcome with emotion and grateful for the answer I had been searching for.

As my daughters looked up again at the handprint against the backdrop of clouds, I noticed we were all smiling, as if we had just discovered a very important clue in the mysteries of life. *Who was here? What curiosity prompted these hands to take a closer look? How can we leave our mark on the world today?*

The proof of life contained in this tiny handprint made me reflect on my own lasting impact and the evidence of my awakening. The old me would have dismissed the urge to look up, dismissed the urge to pull over, and most certainly would have been annoyed by the messy handprint. But today, by being open to the possibilities outside of my expectations, this unique little imprint made its way into a routine part of our day and offered a new, healing truth:

Letting go of perfection helps us see what really matters

I now knew the small, tangible shift I needed to recover my joy was possible through a posture of acceptance. By following rather than resisting the urge to stop and pay attention, something remarkable became available to me.

Acceptance would become the bridge from the painful truth of "I am sacrificing my joy and peace to hold up a facade" to living out a new truth: "Letting go of perfection helps me see what matters."

Just think of what might happen if I accept more and resist less, I thought to myself excitedly.

With time and practice, I began to see that accepting what "is" over what "isn't" actually reduces fear, doubt, worry, and anxiety, opening up opportunities for unexpected outcomes. Choosing acceptance is an intentional act that expands our view, enabling us to experience joy in ways we couldn't before.

I began cultivating a mindset of acceptance with minor issues, which laid the groundwork for navigating bigger issues later. Here are a few examples of my shift in perspective around less consequential issues:

> "I can't get this stain out of my shirt, but it would be silly to discard it because of this small flaw. It's still comfortable and goes with my favorite pants."

> "The doctor is running late, but this gives me time to process my thoughts since I don't have anywhere else to be."

> "The towels were not folded the way I like, but they were folded, and I had time to enjoy some reading."

> "I burned the dinner rolls, but my family got the opportunity to demonstrate grace and flexibility by slicing off the burnt part and assuring me that it wasn't a big deal."

Accepting small inconveniences enabled me to see positive outcomes even when they weren't initially obvious. I called this practice "seeing flowers, not weeds."

Eventually, this perspective began to shift to people. Here are a few examples:

"Natalie made a mess making scones but look at what she created. I don't think I would have done something that adventurous at her age."

"Avery is taking forever to put on her pj's, but look at how she relishes the smell of clean pajamas—I will savor this moment with her."

"Scott didn't ask me about the manuscript I just submitted, but he can't read my mind. I will tell him how difficult this project was for me and that I want to celebrate it."

As I continued to practice this mindset change, I was also able to reflect with more loving eyes on characteristics I had longed to change in myself. My sensitive side that I previously judged for being too emotional and introverted was also what enabled me to feel life so deeply. I realized it was that part of me that allowed me to write what others felt but often couldn't express.

Like that dirty handprint on the glass, I began to see great significance in the imperfect, the unplanned, and the unbecoming of what was expected. This new perspective led me to have greater transparency with my family around internal struggles that were difficult to share.

As a parent, we don't always get confirmation that our messages are having the intended impact, but my choice to be upfront about my insecurities was affirmed when the COVID-19 global pandemic began.

My daughter Natalie, who was seventeen at the time, had a much more astute awareness of the toxic messaging and superficial measurements of worth circulating in our culture than I did. When fear during the initial months of the pandemic caused life to feel like it was spiraling out of control, Natalie noticed me falling back into old patterns, reverting to controlling and damaging coping mechanisms, which in my case often manifested in how I judge and treat my physical self.

Natalie recognized that I was struggling and knew what I needed. On Christmas morning she handed me a gift: inside the plain brown paper tied with a teal ribbon was a framed, hand-lettered list of body positive affirmations written by Brittany Woodard, Registered Dietitian Nutritionist.

Initially, I panicked and felt exposed. I thought, *Oh no. Natalie sees my struggle, and now everyone else will, too.*

My parents, who were watching via Zoom, asked me to read the art out loud, while Scott and Avery nodded enthusiastically.

I took a deep breath and remembered, *I don't have to hide my weaknesses and insecurities. That is not who I am anymore. I am a human being who bears her scars, a human being who knows healing happens in community, a human being who knows life is not meant to be navigated alone.*

With my bravest voice, I read all the affirmations out loud as my family listened:

My size is not my worth.

I am allowed to fuel my body with food.

I am enough, just as I am now.

I can trust and listen to my body.

I don't need to change my body for others.

My body is worthy of love.

I love my body for what it helps me do.

Vocalizing these healing beliefs in the presence of my family felt like an exhale I'd been waiting for decades to release. Because, when I looked up, my family seemed unmistakably pleased that I could now perceive myself the way they had seen me all along: perfectly imperfect.

When we let go of perfection, we see what really matters, which eventually translates to *living what matters out loud* so we—and others around us—can experience the kind of connection that offers true acceptance and healing.

We do this through one small act of acceptance at a time. As we have talked about in previous areas of exploration, it is the small, intentional shifts—not massive overhauls—that create the positive and lasting transformation we seek.

STEPPING-STONE ONE
(A PLACE TO JUST BE)

Dear Soul Shift Companion, in order to prepare for a Practice in Letting Go of Perfection, it's necessary to recognize that **acceptance is a way of being that is initiated by choice**.

Perhaps you can think of a time in your life when you chose to accept what was (rather than cling to what wasn't) and it led to an unexpected, desirable result. Simply thinking about that experience is an act of preparation for creating healthy shifts in your life. Why? Because changing your mindset begins with awareness. To help, I have provided six statements that may serve as a springboard for greater understanding of any perfectionistic inclinations you may have. These statements are likely to touch tender places inside you, indicating there is information waiting there to lead and enlighten you. As tender as it may feel to explore these areas, please resist the urge to rush or distract yourself; sit with whatever feelings these statements bring to the surface and reflect on what your reaction is trying to tell you.

- I constantly feel like I am falling short.

  How does this statement make you feel? Does it resonate? Does it bring pain to the surface? What situations or people make you feel most insecure about not measuring up?

- If I reveal my flaws and imperfections, I will be rejected.

  How do you feel when you read that statement? Is there a part of you that believes this to be true? If so, why do you think that is?

- My value comes from what I achieve or what I do for other people.

  Is there a sense of familiarity in this belief? What rings true about it? When did this belief begin? Did certain circumstances condition this thinking?

- It's hard for me to take criticism—it feels like a judgment about my worth or ability.

  Is this true for you? In what way?

- If I want something done right, I have to do it myself.
  Can you identify with this statement? Do you have a hard time trusting others to care enough or do things as well as you? Is this a pressure you feel in a particular area of your life? How so?

- If I make a mistake, I have a hard time letting it go.
  What feelings come up when you read that statement? Do you replay a specific mistake in your head? Does your inner voice respond with shame or embarrassment?

If any of these statements brought uncomfortable feelings to the surface, this is not a moment to judge yourself; it is a moment to be proud of yourself for taking some critical steps forward to gain insight into the tendencies you have that fuel self-limiting beliefs and strain your relationships. By leaning into this process of self-reflection, you are preparing yourself to choose more helpful and loving responses in triggering situations.

STEPPING-STONE TWO
(A PLACE TO BECOME AWARE)

Dear Soul Shift Companion, the process of recovering your joy through a posture of acceptance begins with a starting point. You can start right here, right now, by being open to the possibilities outside of your preconceived expectations. The following check-in questions have no right or wrong answers; you are in a no-judgment zone. The purpose here is to assess where you are right now so you can figure out which direction will take you where you most want to go. By following, rather than resisting, the guidance of your heart, useful information for your journey can become available to you here.

1. Do you have trouble meeting your own standards in terms of body image, performance, or productivity? Do you think your loved ones feel like they have trouble meeting your standards? What are the costs of these standards?

2. Do you often hear yourself say, "You should . . . ?" If the answer is yes, does that pressure or expectation interfere with what you really want to do or who you really want to be? How so?

3. If you gave yourself permission to release control and/or lower expectations, what opportunities do you think might open up for you? Can you describe a specific scenario?

STEPPING-STONE THREE
(A PLACE TO PREPARE THE WAY)

If your responses reveal your tendency to choose a state of resistance over acceptance, celebrate this valuable awareness and assure yourself that, yes, **it is possible** to shift your current way of thinking. Establishing an open mindset and a willingness to overcome self-limiting beliefs happens through a Practice in Letting Go of Perfection, which starts with acceptance.

Eleven years ago, I never would have believed I could overcome my critical and controlling ways, but I did, and it began with the decision to accept Scott's painful observation that my soul recognized as truth.

"You're never happy anymore"—those four words I didn't want my daughters to hear were ones I later shared, nervously, with an audience of one thousand people.

Scott had come to the event to support me and was by my side at the post-conference meet and greet.

One of the attendees approached us and asked if she could say something to Scott.

"That must have been really hard for you to say to Rachel. But I am so grateful you did, because it spurred Rachel's healing journey, and now Rachel is spurring mine."

When the woman embraced me, I thought, *Isn't this what it's all about?*

Isn't it when we stop portraying a fake image of ourselves that we make authentic connections?

Isn't it when we open the doors to our messy lives that joy, laughter, and love can find their way in?

Isn't it when we show each other our scars that we love each other more?

I think so. Therefore, I plan to live out my life standing in the light of truth and authenticity, and I will embrace anyone who courageously meets me there.

Would you like to meet me there? If so, please take my hand.

STEPPING-STONE FOUR
(A PLACE TO STEP OUT)

Dear Soul Shift Companion, it is time to begin your Practice in Letting Go of Perfection. In this territory, the habit shift is VALIDATION.

This actionable step for a Practice of Letting Go of Perfection is based on a light-bulb moment provided by my dear friend and renowned Language of Listening coach, Sandy Blackard.

Early in my career as an author, I reached out to Sandy when one of my readers asked me how to best support her perfectionist child.

These are the life-changing words Sandy wrote:

> You can do that by validating her need to be perfect, because to her it is extremely important, if not urgent, to be perfect. I know it may sound backwards, but from a perfectionist child's point of view, being told it is okay to mess up, show emotion, and not care what her friends think is telling her she is wrong to be herself, even if that is not your intention.
>
> Here's why: the normal human reaction to being told you are wrong is to become defensive and prove that you are right. You are proving it to yourself as much as to the person who criticized you, tried to fix you, or told you that you were wrong.

Acceptance is the missing element in shifting perfection-ism from an anxiety-ridden behavior to a gift of excellence. Once she knows it's okay to be the way she is (no matter what that is), she can naturally start to relax about it.

Sandy's wisdom confirmed what I was beginning to see on my own—that in order to let go of perfection (or in my case, the fear of not being enough), I needed to validate myself. Over time, I have discovered three practical ways to do this: verbally, emotionally, and progressively. As I lead you through these three forms of validation, be thinking about which form you'd like to begin practicing today as your Letting Go of Perfection habit shift.

1. Verbal Validation

When I made the decision that my fear of inadequacy would not stop me from grasping the moments that mattered, I realized there were three situations that triggered my perfectionistic tendencies. In order to move through them, I established self-compassionate statements and found it helpful to actually say them out loud.

Dr. Jason Moser, a researcher on the positive impact of verbalizing self-talk, explains why: "Referring to yourself in non-first person pronouns or your own name leads people to think about themselves more similarly to how they think about others, and you can see evidence for this in the brain. This process helps people gain a tiny bit of psychological distance from their experiences, which can often be useful for regulating emotions." Here are some examples of some of the rough terrain that can be triggering for me and the verbal validations I have learned to offer myself.

- Caring "too much" about a project I am passionate about is an area in which I feel both shame and overwhelm. The following statement helps me practice compassion: "You are working really hard because this project is important to you. Wanting to do quality work is nothing to be ashamed of. Just remember, rest is a vital part of the process of completing this project."

- Being hyperfocused on how other people are going to respond to something I create or present is a perfectionistic tendency that I put into perspective with this loving statement: "Rachel's job is to show up. Period. It is not her job to know how this is going to turn out or how she will be received."

- Advocating on issues of social justice and racism is an area in which I fear making a mistake. This powerful validation enables me to stay committed and engaged: "You decided that staying silent is not an option for you, and making mistakes is part of this vital work. If you mess up, you'll take ownership and then you'll keep going with a willingness to learn."

Practicing verbal validations out loud not only helped me move through difficult moments I encountered, it also helped members of my family know how to better help each other through tense moments. In our home, unhelpful statements like, "Calm down . . . It doesn't have to be perfect . . . Why are you so stressed about this?" have been replaced by one simple statement that makes struggling people feel seen, heard, and supported: "How can I help?"

The second type of validation that helps me shift me from perfection and control to peace and trust is . . .

2. Emotional Validation

As I was learning to accept all parts of myself, including my insecurities and weaknesses, I made another breakthrough: fear wears disguises.

This realization came to me during a whitewater rafting trip. Terrified that Avery was going to fall out of the raft, I began calling out orders, sharp and gruff. Scott told me not to be upset, to which I responded, "I'm not mad; I'm scared. This is fear talking."

Later, when tucked safely inside our cabin, I reflected back on my words. Suddenly, I was able to see the unbecoming behaviors that I'd exhibited for decades in a new, forgiving light. I'd often wondered why I mistreated and tried to control people I loved so much. Attributing those unbecoming behaviors to fear of rejection, failure, and loss helped me pull back the shame so I could offer myself a new response when I found myself getting mean, controlling, and defensive.

With this insight, I'd pause and ask myself: *Is there something else going on? What feels out of control for you right now? Would it help to tell someone how you are feeling?*

Pausing to address the underlying cause of my outburst doesn't always work, but when it does, I am reminded that what I—and most people—need in our most difficult moments is validation and understanding, not rejection or shame.

The third form of validation that has the power to loosen perfection's grip is . . .

3. Progressive Validation

As I mentioned earlier, accepting little things that didn't go as planned led to my ability to accept upsets with bigger consequences. In fact, I was astonished by two painful situations I was able to accept. The first one was having my plantar fasciitis become so severe that I had to stop taking walks for many months to have surgery and fully heal. The second was accepting the abrupt ending of a dear friendship with no explanation.

In both instances, I realized I had two choices: I could hold onto the way things were (though I knew resisting the flow of life only made me unhappy) or I could accept things for how they were and use my energy to invest in healing, connecting, and growing.

In each of these instances, the posture of acceptance led to new opportunities—I couldn't take walks, but I found enjoyment from daily swim sessions with Avery. My friend was no longer accessible to me, but I was able to grow closer to a new friend with whom I could be my authentic self.

Dear Soul Shift Companion, in the days and weeks ahead, there will be times when things do not go as planned and the need for control or perfection will grip you. Set an intention right now to demonstrate acceptance by writing down which validation you feel most inclined to use.

When you use it, come back and document it on your map. Know these acts of acceptance will lead to more significant surrenders that will bring unexpected joy and peace to your life.

This shift begins with one choice, one gesture of acceptance of the way things *are* instead of the way you may want them to be. Let's commit to this intention by making our visual reminder. Grab a sticky note and write down the healing truth that we uncovered today:

A PEACEFUL SPOT

(a Place to Let Things Sink In)

Stories:

ACCEPT WHERE YOU ARE

ACCEPT WHERE YOU'VE HURT

ACCEPT WHERE YOU'RE HEALING

Accept Where You Are

"I'm not where I want to be."

I found myself saying those words a lot as I recovered from foot surgery.

They were interspersed between comments my doctor made, like these: "You'll be in the boot for four to six weeks." "We won't know for a few weeks if the procedure worked or not." "Healing will be slow."

I sat on the back deck with my throbbing foot elevated. I hoped that being outside would enhance my current situation. Within arm's reach was a gigantic stack of files for a major project I was working on. Beside it was a writing calendar I'd created to ensure I'd meet my deadline.

"I'm not where I want to be," I said to myself for the thirty-seventh time that day, referring to both my physical state and my project status.

I knew I was not alone in my disappointment. As I looked up at the blue sky overhead, one struggle after another came to mind.

I thought about Avery, who had just graduated from middle school. Instead of feeling excited about the completion of this chapter in her life, she felt worried. An unconventional and isolating eighth grade year of virtual learning resulted in poor choices with less than desirable outcomes.

"I am not where I want to be."

I thought about my friend packing her suitcase as she prepared to take her kids to the beach for the first time in their lives. She confided to me how deeply she yearned to embrace her body that had changed dramatically over the past year.

"I am not where I want to be."

I thought about the wastewater spilling into the environment near my parents' Florida home. My parents shared their concern about the ramifications of this leak on the area residents and wildlife. From their retirement home, they were writing letters to government officials, pleading for corrective and protective measures for the world their grandchildren will inherit from them.

"I an not where I want to be."

I thought about George Floyd, his family, and the worldwide movement sparked by his murder in 2020. Although the consciousness of many had been raised, it was becoming quite evident that conversations about racial justice and antiracism education had not led to any real progress to ensure Black lives were valued, protected, and liberated.

Individually and collectively, we are not where we want to be.

That was the recurring theme as I sat on my back deck, unmoving and in pain, attempting to work and heal in nature's office.

For five solid days, the magnitude of everything that needed to be overcome felt immense. Being stuck in one place only added to my hopelessness.

When Scott came outside to check on me, he immediately noticed the music blaring through the thick patch of trees behind our house.

"What is *that*?" he asked, perplexed.

"Every morning at eleven o'clock, the parent and her toddler have a dance party. 'Shake It Off,' 'Party in the USA,' 'Run the World (Girls),' and 'Celebrate Good Times.' Every day. Same time. Same four songs," I explained.

Just then, the parent belted out, "Who runs the world?" and the toddler squealed, "GIRLS!"

Scott and I burst out laughing.

"I can't be mad at them for distracting me from my work," I admitted. "I mean, just listen to that joy."

As Scott turned to go, he paused. "This seems like the kind of thing you would write about . . . you know, so someone else can hear it, too."

When he closed the door, I tearfully considered his thought. The joyful duo was now celebrating good times with Kool & the Gang. That was when a new thought occurred to me:

She's where she wants to be . . .

that little girl

in this moment,

dancing with her mom.

Everything is exactly as it is supposed to be.

I felt a sense of relief in my chest. The heaviness I'd been feeling for days began to ease. That beautiful, hopeful thought came to mind because I was there, parked in a place I did not want to be, but open to the opportunity it presented. Not only did being stuck there allow me to witness this tangible joy between a parent and child, but I also had the ability to spread it.

Before choosing my words to document the wonderous sound, I referred to an inspiring directive written by author and speaker Krystle Cobran, who served as the first-ever Diversity, Equity, and Inclusion officer for the Athens-Clarke County (Georgia) Unified Government. Although Krystle has experienced the brutality of racism and acknowledges the long road ahead, she still believes in what can be. In her April 2021 newsletter, Krystle wrote:

> Sometimes, in the midst of sorrow, the most significant choice we can make is to stay in it. Stay in the journey, stay in the conversation, stay in the pathway of discovery, stay in the learning, stay in the listening, stay in the willingness to make conscious choices. Stay willing to keep beginning—so we can move toward growth, even as we navigate pain.
>
> Stay.

Thanks to a celebratory dance party and Krystle's healing directive, I saw the restrictive boot on my foot in a new light. It showed me that even in the most confined and desolate circumstances, incremental movement is still possible and still impactful when we choose not to give up.

As painful as it is to take another step in this world some days, would you stay the course with me, **dear Soul Shift Companion**?

Although you might not be able to see it right now, there is joy on the other side of the trees. Listen . . . and believe it is within our reach.

Notes to Ponder

I accepted I was not where I wanted to be when . . .

When I pause and imagine what "joy on the other side of the trees" looks like, I see . . .

Accept Where You've Hurt

To avoid working on my 65,000-word manuscript, I procrastinated by removing all the trinkets on our living room bookshelf and replacing them with good books that should never be kept inside drawers and cabinets.

Once the books were arranged, I noticed there was one that really stuck out.

I considered putting it back in the drawer. After all, it wasn't aesthetically pleasing like the other books. But that's not really why I wanted to remove it. I knew it meant I might have to own it.

It only took five days for Avery to notice it.

"*Anti-Diet*? Owned by the person always on a diet?"

Avery spoke with genuine curiosity . . . well, and maybe a touch of animosity. It was exactly what I feared would happen.

"Yes, I'm reading it . . . slowly," I began. "It's a lot to wrap my brain around because it's requiring me to unlearn beliefs that are deeply engrained, like food having moral value and body size determining worth . . . all the damaging beliefs I grew up with."

". . . That you passed on to me," she added without missing a beat.

In that moment, I knew I had a choice. I could make excuses by describing the impact of diet culture on my health and well-being. I could dig in my heels until my daughter saw my side of things. I could explain that when I offered suggestions, I had nothing but good intentions.

But what I've learned though a posture of acceptance is this: no matter how "good" my intentions were, I need to listen when someone tells me the impact was harmful.

There was only one appropriate response to my daughter's remark.

"I know," I admitted. "I now see the harm I caused, and I'm so sorry. I'm trying not to do that anymore."

My child's face softened. In her eyes, I could see that she saw me fully—my struggle, my regret, my mistakes, my humanness. Through my transparency, Avery was invited to put down her defensive shield on this important topic and see hope for new, healing pathways.

While I can't change the past for me or for my daughter, I *can* change the future by releasing the weight of damaging beliefs I no longer need to carry. Do you wish to unload harmful beliefs that have hindered you and those you love?

We can begin by acknowledging the stuff we feel most inclined to keep hidden away. I was scared to leave the anti-diet book on the shelf, where everyone could see it. Because then everybody could see me, too. However, I also knew that displaying it openly on the shelf would help hold me accountable to its message. Because things we keep hidden away are harder to heal and easier to pass on to those we love. But when we allow others to see us, we allow them to love us, too.

Notes to Ponder

I accepted where I hurt (or caused hurt) when . . .

Something I am trying to unlearn is . . .

Accept Where You're Healing

The best way to describe the day I was having was a "Let Down Day." As in, I felt like I was letting people down.

I messed up an important shipment.

I didn't finish my proposal on time.

I didn't get to the post office like I promised.

I couldn't even get myself dressed.

"It's okay," my nurturing voice gently assured me as afternoon turned into evening. "You are tired . . . and these things can wait."

Despite my progress, my former inner productivity manager still raises her voice with some unhealthy commentary from time to time, and she wasn't convinced. My long-held fear of not being enough managed to get some leverage, bringing my greatest insecurities to the surface. Thinking about letting people down had the power to pull me under.

"Go outside," my nurturing voice said, knowing that fresh air and open skies were an instant stress reliever. But it was extremely cold, and I was still in my pajamas. I couldn't fathom mustering the energy to get dressed.

I looked around the kitchen for an alternative option. That's when I spotted our typically rambunctious rescue cat, Paisley, fast asleep. He was curled up in his unconventional "bed," a fruit bowl on the counter, which he chose over multiple cat cushions and soft blankets.

Paisley was healing from the surgical removal of a large mass from his back. When I gently checked his sutures, he started to purr. I couldn't help but lean in and listen to the comforting sound that indicated he was overcoming this unexpected and traumatic event in his young life.

"It's okay to have a down day," I said to him softly.

As my hand rested on his little head, I felt as though someone was placing a loving hand on *my* head—not just to assure me that I have loved this odd cat well, but also to assure me that I am loved as he is loved, that it is, indeed, "okay to have a down day."

With that, I breathed a sigh of relief. Perhaps my Let Down Day was not about letting other people down at all; perhaps it was about letting down my defenses, my expectations, and my protective walls so there, in my raw and vulnerable state, love could reach my most tender places.

Notes to Ponder

I accepted where I am healing when . . .

If I were to create a "Let Down Day" list of things that bring me comfort and ease, I would include . . .

ASSURANCE FOR YOUR POCKET

May you embrace your enoughness
when you are missing something
when you have everything you need
when you are anxious about the future
when you have all your ducks in a row.

May you embrace your enoughness
when you raise your voice in desperation
when you suffer in silence
when you are rejected
when you are loved.

May you embrace your enoughness
when you show up flanked by friends
when you hold your own hand
when you feel ill-prepared
when you feel capable of taking on the world.

May you embrace your enoughness
when you can't tell a soul
when you say too much
when you can't escape the darkness
when sunlight warms your face.

May the false measurements of "enoughness" release from
your skin.
May your true indicators of worth grow like wings.
May you rise up, using this truth as your power:
*showing up, no matter how hard the circumstances or how
ill-prepared I feel, is what makes me enough.*

PRACTICE FOUR
BEING KIND TO YOURSELF

START HERE . . .

I wish you peace from a harsh inner voice,
a softer message, choice by choice.

I wish you peace from mistakes inhabiting your mind,
a perspective of grace that's there to remind.

I wish you peace from wounding beliefs blocking your view,
an untainted glimpse of the beauty in you.

And through each inner triumph, may you discover a new way,
a wide, open path marked, "Only love today."

May affirming signs be evident and clear,
overpowering the pull of shame and fear.

At last, a healing transformation will begin,
rooted in self-love, blossoming from within.

Learning self-love is an essential part of cultivating a life that matters to you. Self-love is rooted in compassion and is the foundation of lasting joy, inner peace, and soulful connections.

My hope is that after exploring this practice area with me, you'll have gained awareness about one of the major ways we deflect love—by being hypercritical. Our inner voice provides the narrative we use to filter information, shape perspective, and make decisions, so an unhealthy internal dialogue can wreak havoc on our lives in subtle and even unconscious ways. It undermines our self-perception, confidence, and performance, and negatively impacts our relationships and our general outlook on life.

The critical inner voice is not a figment of our imagination; it is responsible for activating the negative internal commentary and damaging thoughts that often speak on our behalf and work against us, discouraging us from acting in our own best interest. There are several theories about where our critical inner voice originates, but a common belief is that it is shaped by destructive early life experiences such as judgment, shame, or the message that we aren't physically, emotionally, or behaviorally "good enough." We don't know how to process those feelings at a young age, so we accept and internalize the narrative as true, and in time, begin to develop coping mechanisms for those feelings. Although it is helpful to consider the origins of our inner critic, it is important to remember that *we* are the ones who now get to decide if we continue to allow and feed these debilitating messages in the present day and beyond.

It's not easy to rewrite the script, especially if we have been rehearsing it for decades, so learning to distinguish when your inner voice is talking is a crucial first step to cultivating a Practice in Being Kind to Yourself. Recognizing your inner critic's voice puts you in the right position to begin challenging what it is telling you. With practice, this empowering new freedom will help you to rebuild a healthier inner voice capable of isolating the former feelings of inadequacy and replacing them with messages of support and compassion.

There's a good chance you are not fully aware of how harmful your inner voice is. I know I wasn't. It wasn't until I began listening to my body through my Practice of Presence that I realized how much destruction was going on inside me. Learning to identify how negative internal comments made me feel helped me see that my reactions to external responses were motivated by the pressures I felt from those feelings. Grasping this truth helped me begin to understand that I was responsible, not the external factors I often blamed, for the unrelenting pressure I felt.

As you will learn in the pages ahead, my destructive thought process didn't just affect me; it also impacted my loved ones. Yet, despite living under its control for decades, it wasn't too late for me to neutralize my inner critic so I could decide for myself how I wanted to show up in the world.

If the presence of a critical internal dialogue feels familiar but overcoming it feels daunting, know that you are right where you need to be. The first step to transformation is just showing up, and you are here. Thank you for being willing to take this important step toward awareness of—and control over—your inner critic.

I'd like to take you now to the point in my journey where my narrow road of self-judgment ended and the open sky of self-compassion beckoned . . .

I grew up hearing the words, "Be kind to others."

What I didn't often hear: "Be kind to yourself."

I probably could have used more of that. The truth is, despite the bright smile I wore on my face and the success I experienced as I matured, the voice in my head was critical and harsh. My inner bully said things like:

"I can't go out looking like that."

"I'm not really good at this. I should just give up."

"I have nothing worthwhile to contribute. I should just stay quiet."

"I don't fit in here."

"What is wrong with me?"

These internal judgments constantly held me back from meaningful life experiences. They also triggered negative moods, which spilled out onto the people I loved.

At a particularly stressful period in my life there was one person who bore the brunt of my critical reactions, and that was my first-born daughter, Natalie.

I can still picture the moment vividly in my mind; seven-year-old Natalie had gotten on a stool and was reaching for something in the pantry when she accidently knocked over an entire bag of rice. As one thousand tiny grains pelted the floor, I saw a look of fear in her eyes that brought me to my knees.

My child made an innocent mistake, and she is terrified of my reaction, I thought, feeling horrified and ashamed. *Is this how I want her to grow up? Is this the parent and person I want to be?*

As Natalie and I worked together to pick up the spilled rice, I was tempted to push these painful questions away, but instead I allowed myself to acknowledge them. Through that posture of acceptance, a painful truth surfaced: **I judge myself, and as a result, I judge my child. This behavior will not only destroy our relationship, but it will rob us both of our peace, purpose, and joy.**

As you can imagine, this realization was extremely painful and difficult to admit, but it helped me see the damaging impact of my internal dialogue and provided the motivation I needed to change the way I spoke to myself. I wasn't sure how to make that shift, but I felt certain that learning to speak more compassionately to myself would also influence how I spoke to those I love.

My first step in making that shift became clear one morning during my Practice of Presence.

Only love today.

That is the phrase that popped into my head as I was praying and journaling.

Thinking that phrase could effectively neutralize my inner bully, I immediately wrote it down on a sticky note and posted it on my bathroom mirror.

Within minutes, I had a chance to use it.

My inner critic started berating my appearance, and I promptly detached myself from my tormenting faultfinder with "only love today."

It worked! The stream of disparaging comments stopped long enough for me to finish getting dressed.

I used that same strategy multiple times throughout the day. Whenever I caught a critical thought coming to my mind or out of my mouth, I'd immediately challenge it by saying those three words, often out loud: "Only love today."

Now, I'll admit I found myself saying the mantra VERY frequently—I nearly sounded like a broken record—but the impact was evident. Within days of utilizing the phrase, I was responding more patiently and kindly to my children and to myself.

Those three empowering words—"only love today"—temporarily neutralized the bully in my head and enabled me to take control. I could then consciously decide to reject the inner bully's self-limiting directives and push beyond the narrative to accomplish things that were important to me.

Over time, I was not only able to identify and overcome my inner bully, I was also able to revise its negative messages with realistic and compassionate truths.

"I can't go out looking like that" became "The people I am meeting today love me for ME—not my appearance. I will be missed if I don't go."

"I am failing my kids" became "Our family is going through a rough time, and despite the stressors, I am showing up."

"I shouldn't be so insecure" became "The deepest need of the human heart is to belong, so wanting to be accepted simply means I am human."

As I began to respond more compassionately to myself, I realized my inner critic was just a really scared part of me trying to protect me from being hurt or rejected. Those disparaging thoughts were the product of old beliefs I'd carried for years and years. But the person I was becoming knew that appearance, status, salary, and popularity are not what make human beings worthy of showing up. We are worthy of showing up because there is no one else in the entire universe who has our unique contribution to make.

It felt truly momentous to participate in meaningful life experiences that my scared, inner critic had previously denied me from experiencing. Yet nothing could compare to the joy I felt after witnessing the impact my internal shift had on Natalie. My parents articulated the transformation in an unforgettable email response to a photo of Natalie tending to her backyard garden. Captivated by the peace on her face, I'd snapped a picture from the kitchen window and sent it to my parents.

This was their response:

> Thank you for this precious picture of our beautiful granddaughter. Over the last two years, we have seen a tremendous change in her. We no longer see a scared look in her eyes; she is less fearful about you being upset or impatient with her. She is much happier and more relaxed. She is thriving and growing into a content, creative, and nurturing person. We know for a fact the changes we see in her coincide with the changes we have also seen in you.

It was while reading my parents' observation that a new, healing truth came to me: **when we are kind to ourselves, we create peace.**

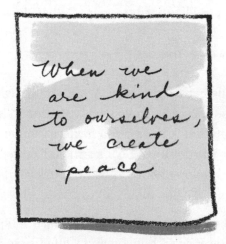

I wish someone had told me to be kind to myself when I was younger—but it wasn't too late. It wasn't too late for me, and it wasn't too late for the people I love. It's not too late for you either, my friend.

STEPPING-STONE ONE
(A PLACE TO JUST BE)

Dear Soul Shift Companion, I'm sure you have already begun thinking about your own internal dialogue, and perhaps you are already aware of how damaging it is. Neutralizing our inner critic can be hard work. It can be challenging and painful to acknowledge debilitating thoughts and make the shift to a more compassionate inner dialogue. But remember, there is great power in one positive choice. By choosing just one loving response that nurtures a sense of support and acceptance rather than criticism, you plant a seed of compassion with the power to grow far beyond what you once thought possible.

A vital step in preparing for this shift on our journey is to establish your perception of your inner voice and learn how to recognize when it is speaking. The following descriptions of inner voice, as collected by writer and researcher Jennifer Hodgson during interviews at the Edinburgh International Book Festival in 2014, are enlightening.

The question posed to writers was, "What does your inner voice sound like?"

Here are a few responses:

"I think it's just a thought voice. A voice of thought; it's not a voice of words. I suppose, when you pay attention to it, I suppose it's a bit like meditation in a way: you focus on something. You focus and then the words come. So it's almost like the old days when you used to develop photographs in a dark room and the image would emerge; it's like that."

"I don't have an inner voice. My inner voice is not at all different from my outer voice. I don't spend a lot of time thinking x and saying y. I will occasionally hear the voice of one of my late parents, or a teacher I was very close to."

"It's a really hard question to answer. I mean, I have a really rich inner life all the time . . . I think the days that I just don't ever talk to myself are kind of wasted days . . . I am talking to myself all the time, and sometimes all that mundane stuff, just *I have to check my email* or *I wonder are the kids up*, or *What time does the store close?*, you know."

Notice the ambiguity of each participant's interpretation of their inner voice. There is no hard or fast rule about what an inner voice sounds like or is *supposed* to sound like, so be assured your own interpretation can be anything—and is right for you. Maybe your internal voice is a feeling, like getting an inner nudge to do something or reach out to someone. Maybe it's the voice of a deceased relative, a past teacher, or a best friend. Maybe it's a running dialogue in your head about what you need to do today. Perhaps it's the voice of a parent or a judgmental voice of authority that you internalized as a child. Maybe it's a combination of several of these, one that varies depending on your circumstances or environment.

Using the thought bubble below, please illustrate in symbols, colors, or words your response to this question: What does your inner voice sound like?

If you found it difficult to describe or illustrate your inner voice, please don't be discouraged. You don't have to know anything with certainty to begin creating the awareness needed to act in more loving ways toward yourself. The most important thing to remember as you move forward is this: No matter what narrative about self-love and kindness you inherited growing up, you now have the awareness and authority to choose what messages you allow to be heard from this point forward. Would you like to choose compassion? Patience? Grace? Acceptance? Love? Then you are in the right place. Let's keep going.

STEPPING-STONE TWO
(A PLACE TO BECOME AWARE)

Dear Soul Shift Companion, to locate the most sensible starting point for your shift to a more compassionate inner voice, I encourage you to assess where you are right now through the process of introspection. Place your hand on your heart and release any expectations you might have about how this process is going to go. Be open, gentle, and curious as you glean valuable information from the check-in questions below.

1. Using the circle below, color in the percent of the time you feel your inner voice is negative or critical toward you. Using the second circle and a different color, indicate what percentage of time you aspire to a compassionate and kind inner voice.

2. Are there certain times or situations when your inner critic is more vocal? Perhaps in front of the mirror, at the start of a certain task, when you are trying to fall asleep, or around a particular person? If so, why do you think these particular people or situations trigger your critical voice?

3. Is there a particular message your inner critic often relays? Have you ever heard this message before, either from someone else or a situation that caused you to feel insecure in the past?

4. When was the last time you spoke words of kindness and compassion to yourself? If it was recent, what did you say? If it's been a while, write down an affirmation that feels applicable for where you are right now. For example: *I am worthy of love and kindness. I can choose loving thoughts toward myself. I am becoming who I am meant to be.*

STEPPING-STONE THREE
(A PLACE TO PREPARE THE WAY)

Dear Soul Shift Companion, if the introspective exercise you just completed felt awkward, confusing, or overwhelming, please remember that this is practice, not perfection. And the purpose of practice is to gain proficiency and become more comfortable doing something new. Let's take a moment to equip ourselves for the Practice in Being Kind to Yourself by visualizing a very important reminder for this work. Humor me and picture the familiar orange and black colors that alert our attention to a construction zone along with a sign that reads "LEARNING GOING ON HERE. PLEASE BE PATIENT."

You may think I am joking about the sign, but I could not be more serious. When Natalie started learning how to drive, we quickly noticed that most fellow drivers were annoyed and frustrated by the slower pace and hesitation that came with inexperience. After a couple of weeks of cars blasting their horn forcing Natalie to feel pressure to proceed before she felt ready, I took to the Internet and ordered an obnoxious fluorescent sign for the car. (Actually, I ordered three to cover more area, but Natalie assured me that one was sufficient.)

"Please Be Patient . . . STUDENT DRIVER," the sign said, sparking compassion and understanding that didn't exist before.

Instantly, the cars behind Natalie gave her space; the honking stopped; the angry hand gestures ceased. Natalie relaxed and was able to learn what she needed to become a capable, independent driver, all because we communicated that we needed space and patience.

Dear Soul Shift Companion, take a moment and imagine a neon sign with encouraging words affixed to your back as you move into the final stretch of this practice area. What does your sign say?

Now . . .

See yourself peering through a cracked windshield.

See yourself making tricky left-hand turns in thick traffic.

See yourself charting a better course for those following behind you.

This is not a time to lay on the horn, let out an exasperated sigh, or increase your speed. This is a time to let your heart soften. Let patience kick in. Allow grace to be your main source of fuel. Such gentle responses will protect and empower you as you allow this journey of reclaiming your joy to unfold.

STEPPING-STONE FOUR
(A PLACE TO STEP OUT)

Dear Soul Shift Companion, it is now time to embark on our Practice in Being Kind to Yourself. The habit shift that provides the bridge from self-sabotage to self-compassion is IDENTIFICATION. By learning to identify your inner critic's voice, you'll be less likely to believe its debilitating lies and follow its destructive advice. You'll be in a better position to replace these messages with realistic and compassionate responses to yourself, even in times of fear, stress, and insecurity.

The following exercise created by Dr. Lisa Firestone is one I come back to again and again, even if it's just going through the process mentally. For today's purposes, I'd like you to use two pieces of paper.

Step 1

Divide a piece of paper in half by either folding it lengthwise or drawing a line down the middle. On the left side of the page, please write down any negative thoughts you've had toward yourself recently.

I will give you an example:

I am so unmotivated lately.

Now, on the right side of the page, translate this same statement into the second person. My statement becomes:

You are so unmotivated lately.

When I read that, I bristle a little. This statement is unkind and unhelpful. It causes the hole to deepen and the spiraling to start. Here's where I find myself going with this:

You are so unmotivated. You are so behind. You can't seem to focus long enough to get anything accomplished. You're going to disappoint everyone.

Whew. Now I am really feeling defeated.

Let's go to Step 2 . . .

Step 2

Take that second piece of paper and place it along the right side of the first one. On this new page, next to the debilitating comment, write a realistic and impartial view of yourself, your qualities, and/or your current situation. Use your own name.

Mine becomes:

Rachel is juggling a lot right now, and it's natural to feel tired. Shame is not a motivator. Grace, compassion, and understanding—that is what will motivate her. She can do that by breaking up tasks and doing one thing at a time.

This process is powerful. By identifying a self-limiting thought and rephrasing it using my name, I am able to put space between the message and myself. This separation allows me to see the statement "I am so unmotivated lately" as being fueled by a societal belief that human beings must always be productive and rest must be earned. Seeing the statement for what it is allows me to reject it, rephrase the message in ways that align with my beliefs about worth, and replace feelings of defeat with hope and reassurance.

Dear Soul Shift Companion, I'd like you to take a moment to go through this process. You may do it on separate sheets of paper or in this guidebook.

Write down a self-judgmental thought in first person, starting with the word *I*:

Translate it to second person, starting with the word *you*:

Turn the statement above into a realistic and impartial view of yourself or situation, using your own name:

The more you practice this process, the more natural it will become. Although it won't be possible to rid yourself of all self-critical thoughts, you can decrease their frequency and shift how you respond to them using the exercises we just explored. The moment when you recognize your nurturing voice has taken root is one you won't forget, especially when it impacts someone you love.

This happened to me when my five-year-old niece, Kate, and her family were visiting from Indiana. It had been a busy morning and Kate said she did not want to go to the community pool with her brothers, aunt, uncle, and cousins.

Kate's statement drew opposition, and well-meaning people tried to convince her to go. I watched as Kate's face became red and agitated.

In that moment, I saw an opportunity. Instead of teaching Kate to power through feelings of exhaustion, I could teach her to love herself through them. Instead of pressuring her to abandon her needs to please others, I could encourage her to honor herself and her limits.

"Kate, would you like to stay home with me and read books in my bed?" I asked.

With a look of relief, Kate tearfully nodded yes.

After reading a couple of books, Kate fell fast asleep. As I laid beside her, I remembered her mom, Stacie, telling me I didn't have to lay with Kate—I could get up and do whatever I needed to do.

In my brain, a whole slew of tasks began circling.

And just when the "you shoulds" nearly convinced me to get up, I said, "Only love today. I am worthy of rest, just like Kate."

For a whole delicious hour, I stayed beside my sleeping niece and read a book.

When Kate woke up and saw me still there, she smiled and thanked me for resting with her, as did my heart.

Dear Soul Shift Companion, the beauty of this journey is recognizing that we have a choice each day. We can work *against* ourselves or *for* ourselves; we can *push* through life or *ease* through life.

I know it's not easy to make the loving choice. We've been conditioned to produce, compete, compare, and consume every minute of every day. We have damaging messages ingrained in our body and embedded in our psyche. But identifying self-limiting dialogue is a catalyst for overcoming it, and we can begin with three powerful words: *only love today.* Love for ourselves is how we'll create change, not just in our own hearts, bodies, and minds, but in our relationships, our communities, and in future generations.

Beloved Soul Shift Companion, please set an intention right now to overcome self-sabotage by writing down a phrase, takeaway, or tool from this practice area that you plan to use right away:

_____

After implementing it in your daily life, be sure to draw a colorful line or symbol on your living map in the back of this guidebook. Every self-compassionate response deepens the healing pathway, eventually making it your favorite footpath, one you know by heart.

Please grab a sticky note and write down the healing truth that we uncovered today. Post this visual reminder where you can see it often.

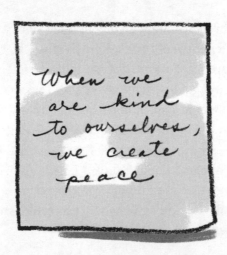

When we are kind to ourselves, we create peace

A PEACEFUL SPOT

(a Place to Let Things Sink In)

Stories:

IDENTIFY YOUR EMOTIONAL ARMOR

IDENTIFY YOUR COMPARISON TRAPS

IDENTIFY YOUR WINDOWS OF RECOVERY

Identify Your Emotional Armor

I wore my BE KIND ball cap to a recent dentist appointment.

This wasn't an accident; I was hoping to send a subliminal message to the person with the sharp, pointed object in her hand *and* feel the security and comfort of a well-worn hat.

Nearly all my adult life, the dentist has been a hard place for me to go. I always enter the office cautious, quiet, and distant. My sensitive self feels unseen at the dentist, so I go in wearing armor.

I am always disappointing someone there—

I never floss enough.

I never open my mouth wide enough.

I cringe too much.

I fidget too much.

The invasive poking and prodding makes me feel defensive.

But this time was different.

The dental hygienist met me in the foyer where patients sat six feet apart. She was covered head to toe in protective gear. All I could see were her familiar blue eyes.

I told her it was good to see her. It wasn't a lie; it was the truth underlined by a new understanding of just what it means to show up as a medical professional in the world today.

Once I was seated in the exam chair, she asked if I was having any issues. I told her about my tooth sensitivity.

I held my breath as the dental hygienist peered inside my mouth, prepared to be shamed for my lack of flossing.

After briefly examining my teeth, she stopped. Before she could say anything to me, I blurted out a vulnerable truth.

"I've been really struggling these past few months," I admitted, blinking back tears. "Finding the energy for even basic oral hygiene has been hard for me."

"I get that," she said genuinely. "Well, the good news is, you're doing good on plaque—no buildup."

The hygienist shared some sensitivity tips and then proceeded to clean my teeth. As she scraped and polished, I focused on the majestic blue whales gliding across the screen above my head.

About fifteen minutes later, she said, "Okay!" Her tone implied the cleaning was finished.

"But what about the carwash for the teeth?" I asked, bracing myself for the agonizing blast. "Or has that type of cleaning been suspended during the pandemic?" I asked, crossing my fingers and toes.

"Well, I prefer not to use it, but there are other hygienists if you wan—"

"Oh no!" I interrupted. "I loved how you cleaned my teeth today! Look, no white knuckles!" I said, holding up my hands and laughing.

"When things go back to normal—whatever that means—you can continue that type of cleaning," the hygienist said, making a note on my chart. "We're reasonable people. All you have to do is tell us," she added.

Oh.

For the second time that day, I teared up, not from pain or shame, but through connection at the deepest human level.

These tender places inside us are so badly bruised that naturally we put up a protective wall. Yet it is that very wall that can keep us from experiencing new, healing outcomes to situations that once brought us pain, fear, and rejection.

After my mouth was rinsed, I commented on the photo sitting in the window. It was not there seven months ago.

"What a beautiful family photo," I said to the hygienist. "How old are your kids now?"

The woman's blue eyes shined through the obtrusive plastic shield as she described the day her daughter's best friend took that photo. She asked about my kids and then went to assist her next patient.

I put on my BE KIND hat but left my defensive armor on the floor.

I liked the idea of fewer walls, more windows, to see and be seen.

Notes to Ponder

I identified a situation in which my
emotional armor was up when . . .

This was helpful because . . .

Identify Your Comparison Traps

I planned to make a special cake for Scott's birthday. Due to circumstances caused by the pandemic, it was the first time in many years that he was home on his actual birthday.

In fact, he'd been working from home for many months and found cooking to be a stress reliever. This was good news and bad news: good because his meals were fabulous; bad because my go-to recipes suddenly tasted bland and uninspired.

For months, I watched in awe as Scott whipped up succulent Crock-Pot recipes in between conference calls. Not to mention he was always freshly showered and wore matching clothes (*overachiever*).

I'd always known Scott was a highly capable guy, but pandemic life uncovered a whole new skill set I didn't know he had. And while he was over there killing it in the midst of so much uncertainty, I found myself struggling . . . a lot.

But there was one area where I knew my skills would not fail me: baking. From a young age, the gooey cookies, muffins, and cakes I made both looked and tasted delicious. Scott's birthday felt like my chance to shine.

Instead of referring to my usual recipes, I used one of Scott's foolproof culinary techniques. By Googling the words "best ever" in front of whatever he wants to make, he finds recipes that live up to their title.

Using Scott's method, I quickly discovered that Ree Drummond, aka "The Pioneer Woman," offered the recipe for "The Best Chocolate Sheet Cake. Ever." After studying the long list of steps, I decided to take it on. Sixteen-year-old Natalie, who had honed her own baking skills during the pandemic, happened to be in the kitchen. I gestured to the recipe, saying how tricky it looked. Unimpressed, Natalie said she didn't think so and took my hesitation as an invitation to hover over me while I baked.

She reminded me to boil the water and questioned the pan I was using. My brand of cocoa powder was also questionable, as was my "heaping" tablespoon. When I thought her commentary was over, she added that it was bad practice to measure the salt over the mixing bowl.

At that point, I had to go to the garage to cool off. I knew that if I stayed in the kitchen any longer, I would blow up.

With arms folded in irritation and hot tears forming in my eyes, I gently asked myself, "Rachel, why are Natalie's efforts to help bothering you so much?"

After a few moments of anguish, I quietly admitted, "I just want to feel capable."

Truth was, I hadn't felt capable at all lately.

Like many people, the stress and disruption of the pandemic threw me for a loop. Even in areas of my life where I typically excelled, I now felt untethered, unmotivated, and inadequate. Each day, in some new way, my long-held fear of not being enough was triggered.

I gently reminded myself that acknowledging these feelings was brave and healthy. In doing so, I was giving myself a chance to address them and perhaps overcome them. I reasoned that expecting myself to function at the same level I did before this world-changing event was self-sabotage. Furthermore, expecting myself to respond to the pandemic the same way other people were responding was also self-sabotage.

I realized that Natalie, in becoming a proficient self-taught baker, was simply eager to show me her skills. I could thank her for her help and tell her how much I wanted to finish the cake by myself.

I came back into the house to find Natalie had gone back to her school-work. I happily heaped, estimated, and taste-tested to my heart's desire. After baking and icing the cake, I placed it proudly on display.

Later that night, our family of four sat around the kitchen table digging into the succulent cake.

I'd hoped to have time to shower for the celebration.

I'd wanted to find matching birthday candles for the cake.

I'd planned to pick out the best surprise gift.

But my limited energy resulted in none of that happening . . . and none of that mattered.

Under the warm glow of the kitchen light, I saw each of us clearly, thriving in new and unexpected ways while floundering in others. I marveled at the fact that the same circumstances had shaped both struggle and growth.

"Growth and healing are fluid processes, not stiff competitions to be won," my nurturing voice whispered.

I promised right then and there to reserve "best ever" status for recipes, not humans. Because when it comes down to it, nothing compares to the best-ever moments—those that happen around the scratched-up kitchen table when we're lucky enough to celebrate another year of life together.

Notes to Ponder

I identified a situation when I was comparing
myself to someone else when . . .

What I did (or plan to do) with this information is . . .

Identify Your Windows of Recovery

I was thrilled to be selected as a "Warm-Down Marshal" for one of Natalie's swim meets during her junior year in high school. (Don't let the title fool you; it sounds way more impressive than it actually is.)

I signed up for one reason and one reason only: to watch my daughter swim. Due to pandemic restrictions, there were no spectators allowed at the swim meet; volunteering was your only way in.

Sign me up!

When I arrived at the aquatic center, I was given an official fluorescent yellow vest. It was just about as stylish as the fanny pack I wore around my waist. I was then told of my duties: stand on the pool deck next to the warm-down pool and make sure the swimmers stay six feet apart.

I breathed a sigh of relief. No map reading, no mathematical calculations, no labor-intensive tasks, just observing. I was made for observing.

As I watched the swimmers exit the competition pool after their first event, I wondered how many would skip the warm down. I mean, I don't know about you, but after swimming 200 yards as fast as humanly possible, I'd be eager to get to my fluffy towel and fortifying snacks.

But the teenage swimmers didn't skip the warm down. Not one of them. I watched them glide through the water with long, easy strokes. Some eventually rested their arms, gently kicking on their backs, eyes fixed to the ceiling as if it were a sky full of stars.

It was one of the most peaceful scenes I'd witnessed in months. Suddenly, I sensed that I wasn't there simply to monitor warm-down lanes and watch Natalie swim. Not knowing yet what that other reason was, I snapped a quick selfie in the neon vest, hoping the image would eventually spark whatever I was supposed to glean from my volunteer position. For added measure, I typed five words into my phone notes: *don't skip the warm down.*

A few days later, after finishing up an intense work project, I thought about the directive I'd typed, and more importantly, witnessed being performed. Rather than moving right to the next task, I decided to pull out several sheets of crisp, white paper to do what my body was telling me I needed to do.

To the teachers of my middle school daughter, I expressed gratitude for the extra patience, guidance, and grace they had extended to her as she struggled in ways she never had before. Them not giving up on her was what kept her hanging on, and they needed to know.

Next, I wrote a testimonial. My therapist, Caroline, whom I'd been working with for eight months, asked me if I would. *Who am I to write a testimonial when my healing is far from over?* I thought skeptically. But as I put pen to paper, the words poured out. Yes, the work was far from over, but Caroline believed in my ability to fully heal. Because of her, I was in a place I never thought I'd be.

And finally, I wrote to a friend to tell her of the void she'd filled in my life. Words I'd tried to say to her for over a year finally found their way to paper. I'd been ashamed to tell her that a trusted friend ghosted me around the same time she'd stepped into my life. She needed to know the light she'd created for me during a very dark time.

As difficult as it was to do these exercises, they were cathartic. I could have skipped them, but then the tightness in my chest from navigating these waters would still be there. I could have skipped them, but then there would be an ache in my bones from failing to acknowledge the special people who had kept me afloat.

It was then that I understood the significance of being a Warm-Down Marshal, a never-needed-before role in the longest and most confusing season in the history of swimming. It was to absorb the words *don't skip the warm down* and apply them to my life.

The world we live in is always so eager to push us forward that we don't get the opportunity to recover—to process, stretch, and stabilize our minds and bodies after enduring a tough event. We miss the chance to say to ourselves, "Remember how scared you were? Remember how you wanted to bail? Remember how you thought about quitting? But you didn't! You made it through."

It is while in this sacred state of restoration and recovery that an ordinary ceiling can look like a sky of stars.

I don't know about you, but I sure don't want to miss that.

Notes to Ponder

I identified a window in which I
could recover from an arduous event or task when . . .

ASSURANCE FOR YOUR POCKET

May these assurances serve as readily available sustenance whenever you need strength.

Stopping to breathe is not unproductive; it's necessary for survival.

Replenishing yourself is not wasteful; it's how you weather the storm.

Asking for help is not weak; it's heeding wisdom to know life is not meant to be navigated alone.

Taking something off your plate is not irresponsible; it's knowing your limits.

Cutting yourself some slack is not silly; it's how you get footing on shaky ground.

May the prickly branches you encounter on your pathway lose their sharp edges with this truth as your hatchet:

Even though it looks unbecoming from where I stand right now, there is a miraculous growth process happening within me. With time, nourishment, and nurturing, there will be blossoms.

PRACTICE FIVE
BEING YOUR
AUTHENTIC SELF

START HERE . . .

If you must give me a gift,
make it one that grows (like a plant) or opens (like a book),
so I can enjoy it for a lifetime of comfort and escape.

If you must give me a compliment,
make it one that goes below the surface,
so I can own it, no matter the ever-changing standards
of beauty.

If you must give me a critique,
make it one that is valid,
so I am not burdened by insecurities of yours being
projected onto me.

If you must give me a hardship,
make it one that is divisible by two,
so I am not forced to carry it alone.

If you must give me a map of directions,
make it one that is open to interpretation,
so I can still rely on my heart for guidance.

If you must give me a hateful viewpoint,
make it one that is lightweight,
so I can fold it into a flower petal and push it out to sea.

If you must give me a goal,
make it one that is doable,
so I can feel encouraged, even with the tiniest of steps.

If you must give me a sliver of time,
make it one rich in connection,
so I can feel held, even as the world spins out of control.

This is my self-reclamation statement.

It took decades of missteps,
a few hard falls,
and some clean breaks . . .
but I got here.

It isn't too late to reclaim yourself.
To say what you will and will not accept
is a good place to start.

Milestone alert! If you have chosen to explore this guidebook in chronological order, then you have reached the halfway point of your Soul Shift discovery journey. It was at this point in my own journey that I began to understand why I'd gotten so far off my truest path in the first place—and why I kept finding it so difficult to recover and reclaim.

It was due to this belief:

> "I must hide certain parts of myself in order to be loved and accepted."

Sometime during my adolescent years, I'd picked up that belief and carried it through a good portion of my adult life. Thankfully, my Soul Shift journey offered experiences that revealed the opposite was true:

> "Showing up in the world as my most authentic self is the only way to experience real connection and true belonging."

Although I am still in the process of learning how to show up in the world as my most authentic self, I've already experienced profound benefits due to steps I've taken to reclaim myself. We'll be taking some of those steps together in the territory ahead.

But before we proceed, I want to clarify something important. This is a safe, nurturing space in which you can explore and discover your authentic self. In this practice area, there are no right or wrong answers. There is no set standard for what it means to live authentically—because living as your truest self is unique to each and every individual.

You are safe to be yourself here.

But who am I? If that thought immediately came to mind, that's okay. I've had to ask myself that question many times. In fact, I believe it's important to periodically ask myself: *Who am I as my most authentic self?*

To help me arrive at an answer, I recall:

It's the version of myself that I embrace when no one else is around.

It's the version of myself in which I feel most safe and comfortable.

It's the version of myself in which my actions align with my beliefs.

It's the version of myself that wears no mask, no persona, no facade.

It's ME at my deepest, truest core.

If the thought of revealing your truest self to others makes you feel apprehensive or vulnerable, that is a very human response. Here is why: letting others see who we really are can feel scary because we know there's a chance we will be rejected.

Maybe you have already experienced pain as a result of revealing your true self, and it's hard to imagine experiencing that again. So why even bother? Why go to the trouble of being who we are if it's only setting us up for the potential of greater pain?

Because the pain of constantly rejecting our inherent self is far greater than any outside rejection we might face.

Pretending to be someone we are not or betraying our values and needs to appease others is exhausting, demoralizing, and unfulfilling.

Living as our most authentic selves, on the other hand, is invigorating, liberating, and naturally rewarding. It allows us to navigate the world in such a way that no matter what someone else says or thinks about us, we see it as an opinion rather than our truth.

Dear Soul Shift Companion, if cultivating a life you actively enjoy instead of merely endure sounds appealing, please lean in as I share the circumstances that led me to a Practice in Being Your Authentic Self. I hope what you read here will help you remove the masks you've acquired over a lifetime so you can embrace who you are and share your gift with the world.

Let's get started.

At the time of my breakthrough to live more authentically, my family was in the process of settling into a new neighborhood. Adding to the anxiety I felt as a newcomer was the blatant emphasis this close-knit community placed on appearance, achievement, and status. Every community event felt like stepping into a fashion magazine photo shoot, and I lacked both the style and the energy to fit in. But for the sake of my daughters and their hopes of finding friends, I made an effort. On one particular day, our family had been invited to a neighborhood gathering, and I really wanted to make a good impression.

On the floor of my bathroom was a pile of discarded outfits. No matter what I put on, I felt unattractive and insecure. I didn't want to arrive late to the gathering and risk having all eyes on me, so I made a snap decision to just settle for something dark and baggy. I headed to my then six-year-old daughter's room, hoping she'd managed to get herself dressed in something acceptable.

I found Avery standing in front of the mirror and immediately noticed how the waistband of her favorite pair of shorts was too snug and clashed with the faded floral shirt she'd chosen. Avery had skipped the hairbrush, opting for a hot pink headband that could not contain her unruly curls.

Just as I was about to open my mouth to tell Avery to change her clothes, I caught a glimpse of her face in the mirror.

The expression reflecting back was one of pure joy. Pure contentment. Pure peace.

When Avery turned and saw me at the doorway, she gave me a glorious smile—a smile that said, "I feel beautiful."

No mask, no facade—nothing but her truest self openly on display.

From deep inside, I heard a fiercely protective voice say, *Let her be.*

Looking back now, I recognize the voice of my Dreamer Girl, my eight-year-old self, who was far more concerned about how things felt than how they looked to others. *Let her be.*

As my Dreamer Girl spoke up for my child, I realized that every time I'd told Avery to change who she was or the way she was showing up in the world, I'd been sending a clear message: *You can't come as you are; you are not enough.*

The last thing I wanted was for my daughter to live in fear of rejection or to make choices based on external approval, as I had done for so long. I wanted her to feel empowered to live, grow, and connect with others on a foundation of truth, courage, and love.

Identifying what I wanted for her allowed me to stay quiet in that pivotal moment and let her go to the community event just as she was.

As her truest, most joyful self in her outfit of choice, Avery joined up with a friend who also had a unique flair and warm energy about him. The duo worked to extract seeds from an apple in hopes of growing a tree. While watching Avery and her friend lost in the joy of their mutual curiosity, I remember thinking, *This is the life I want for her and her friend. I want them to have the space to grow up exactly as they are and not worry about whether who they are is what the world wants to see.*

Truthfully, that life sounded quite appealing to me, too.

But how? And is it too late? I wondered.

The answers came about a year later through a vulnerable conversation with a friend after my daughter's teacher informed me that my child was not progressing as she should. When the school administration spelled out the issues, I was devastated. I couldn't stop feeling like I'd failed my child.

As I was trying to sort things out, my friend happened to call. She could tell I'd been crying and asked what was wrong.

Before I could even think of censoring myself, I blurted everything out.

Much to my surprise, my friend said, "The same thing happened to my son, and I felt like I'd done something wrong, too . . . but Rachel, I didn't . . . and you didn't either. This is part of our children's unique fiber, and because we know them better than anyone else, we are the best guides to help them through their journey."

Suddenly, I felt like a huge weight was lifted; I didn't have to pretend with her. And by admitting what was really going on, my friend and I discovered a common thread that connected us and gave us strength.

Fear had always told me I'd be rejected if I revealed my true self or my true feelings about my struggles, but that wasn't what happened. In fact, I'd never felt more seen or more accepted by a friend in my adult life.

From here, a new, healing truth took root:

I am most available to love and be loved when I show up as my most authentic self.

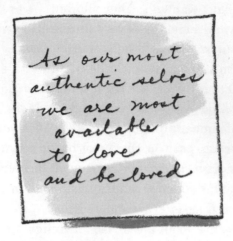

As our most
authentic selves
we are most
available
to love
and be loved

I began to imagine the possibilities. By telling the truth, one person, one difficult moment at a time, maybe I could finally dispel the belief that I must hide parts of myself in order to be loved and could, instead, start living in alignment with my true values, interests, and strengths.

And that was what I did, not knowing at the time that my first step toward being brave and leading with my truth, one interaction at a time, would prepare me to walk alongside my child as she struggled to shape and honor her core identity.

As Avery grew, it became clear that her approach to life was gentler and more intentional than the way the world typically operated. As a deeply empathic human being with both physical and emotional challenges, being her truest self was often painful. I found myself desperately wanting her to "fit in," even pushing her at times to conform. But the more I tried to make my child fit the mold, the more her light diminished.

By the time Avery reached double digits, there was a look of distress on her face every time she left the house. Attributing it to our recent move from a tightly knit community to a large metropolitan area only worked for so long. It soon became impossible to deny that the pained expression on her face seemed to ask, "Am I enough for the world?"

Inspired by the way I was reconnecting with my Dreamer Girl through writing, I thought about where or what might provide Avery space to be and know herself. Music had been Avery's joy and refuge from a very early age, so she and I set up a space in our new home for her to play guitar and sing. This was her space to create music without judgment and critique. I only entered when invited, making a point to simply listen and encourage.

Within a year, Avery decided she wanted to share her musical gift with people. The topic came up during an evening walk as Avery, who was still very homesick, described the hardest thing for her about moving to a new place. Expressing how much she longed to see our old neighborhood where everyone greeted her by name, she said something I'll never forget: "I just want to be known." When I asked where such a place might be, she suggested the nursing home, where people often feel lonely and forgotten.

I distinctly remember the first time we visited our local nursing home. Despite the unpleasant smell, stuffy air, and forlorn faces, eleven-year-old Avery walked in with a purpose. She lovingly greeted each resident sitting in the wheelchairs lining the hallway.

When Avery got out her guitar and began singing "Amazing Grace," low heads rose, dull eyes focused. It was clear that the familiar song stirred something deep inside the residents.

When Avery saw the response of her audience, her voice grew stronger and more at ease. Her face radiated peace and confidence, as if to say, "I'm right where I'm supposed to be."

Naturally, my daughter and I kept visiting the nursing home, leading Avery to learn new genres and styles and eventually try her hand at songwriting. Distinct themes emerged in the lyrics: *it's okay to be different*, *let yourself feel what you feel*, and *you are enough*.

With help from her guitar instructor, Corey, Avery was able to record her original songs and make them available to global listeners through a variety of online streaming services. People of all ages and backgrounds indicated they found peace, solace, and validation through Avery's voice and lyrics.

During the COVID-19 pandemic, Avery began giving virtual lessons to kids her own age. Many of her students struggled socially in traditional settings and found Avery to be an approachable teacher.

After a few months of lessons, a parent of one of her students reached out to me about her son.

"I am sorry he has such a hard time focusing and is probably not progressing as quickly as other students. He loves Avery's lessons and feels so comfortable with her, but we would understand if she doesn't want to teach him anymore."

When I read the message to Avery, she said, "That is not what I see. He catches on quickly. He is very creative and sees things I don't see. I love working with him."

Avery's response confirmed what I was already seeing for myself: When we show up as our most authentic self, differences do not frighten or challenge us. There is no judgment. I honor the authentic you and you honor the authentic me.

I call this phenomenon *meeting in the light of realness* and describe it as a place where belonging is felt, growth is abundant, and purpose is found. Getting there is not easy; it requires being honest with yourself and leaning in when fellow human beings share the realest, rawest version of themselves. But the ones who are willing to allow this level of vulnerability are rewarded with an unmatched feeling of connection and peace.

Dear Soul Shift Companion, would you like to go there? Would you like to discover and cherish what you know to be your innermost self: your gifts, your inclinations, your likes, your dislikes, your fears, your hopes, your dreams? Would you like to reconnect with the uninhibited Dreamer that still exists inside you?

If so, you are exactly where you need to be. Let's keep going . . .

STEPPING-STONE ONE
(A PLACE TO JUST BE)

It's likely you already know that one of the biggest obstacles to living as our most authentic self is the reaction, real or imagined, that we receive from others. While nothing can truly prepare us for the judgment and rejection we may encounter when revealing our true being, we can add some protective armor by reflecting on our options. As a parent of a child with unique wiring and as a former teacher of students who took unconventional paths, these are a few of the choices my former students and my daughter considered when encountering resistance:

- We can either use our time and energy to defend our decisions or nurture our heart-led choices.
- We can either force ourselves to fit into predesigned boxes or create spaces in which we can organically flourish.
- We can either deny our truth to make others more comfortable or act in authentic ways to honor and protect our inner peace.

Here are some prompts to help you think about choices you might have:

- I find myself spending time and energy defending decisions about _____ when I really care about _____ .
- I've felt forced into the box of _____ by _____ but I think I'd really flourish in a space where I could _____ .
- I deny my truth/truest self when I _____ but I'd like to change that and honor myself instead by _____ .

Reflecting on choices like these can help us recognize that we only have so much time and energy; we only have one precious life to live. How do we want to spend it?

My daughter and I have decided we intend to spend it living as our truest selves, so we keep this assurance close when going into challenging situations:

> "We will likely encounter people who won't understand our choice, our approach, or what we need to thrive. But we don't need them to understand; we don't need anyone's approval or permission to do what we know is right for us."

STEPPING-STONE TWO
(A PLACE TO BECOME AWARE)

Dear Soul Shift Companion, living authentically is not static. It is a continually shifting and evolving process. While the authentic path you are setting out on today may not necessarily be the path you stay on, understanding how to locate your most appropriate path will serve you well in life. That is the purpose of this introspective exercise. It is a chance to learn about yourself, challenge old beliefs, and open your mental keepsake box. The following check-in questions are designed to help you reach deeply within yourself and identify what conditions make you feel you can safely express your truest self. Even one small discovery can give you the courage you need to begin living from a place of authentic peace.

1. Is there a place (either in your present life or in your past) where you feel most at home? What about a person whose presence makes you feel like you can breathe? Please describe this place and/or person using as much detail as possible:

2. On a scale of 1 to 10 (1 being never and 10 being always), how often do you share how you're really feeling? To aid the process, mentally go through your day from the minute you woke up to where you are now. Can you think of an example of when you honestly expressed your feelings to yourself or someone else? What was the result? Now, can you think of an example of when you hid your true feelings? What was the result?

3. When is the last time you felt open to *come as you are*? Using the mind map on the next page, illustrate that experience in as much detail as you can. Begin by writing the words "Come as I am" inside the circle. Feel free to add illustrations or symbols around the words. In the extended bubbles, include information such as what the experience felt, sounded, tasted, and looked like. Were there particular words used or certain tones in the voices that spoke to you?

4. The following three prompts are intended to help you uncover important clues about your authentic self that you may have stuffed away due to rejection or judgment. Please give yourself permission to be fully human as you read these prompts and finish them with whatever comes up for you. Extend compassion to yourself and stay curious as you tune into innocent, tender places that haven't been explored or listened to in a while.

When I was growing up, I wanted to be:

When I was _____ years old, I wish I'd had the chance to:

When I was young, I really needed to hear these words:

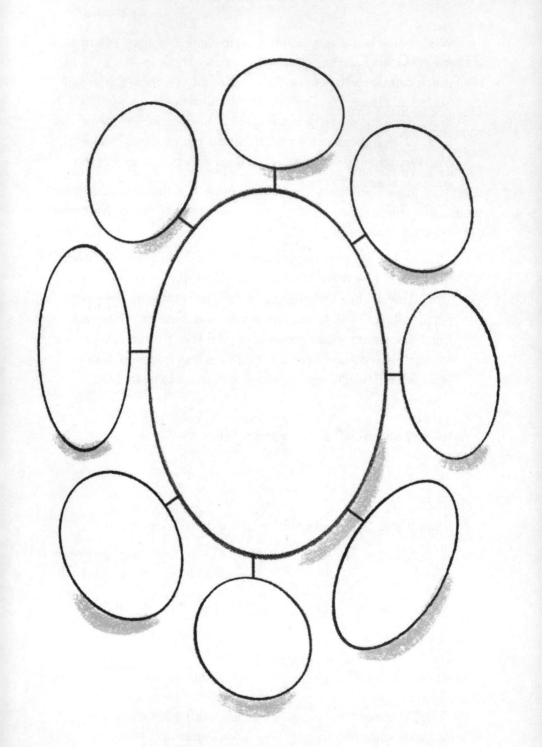

STEPPING-STONE THREE
(A PLACE TO PREPARE THE WAY)

Dear Soul Shift Companion, if responding to these prompts made you emotional, you are in good company. Something about the exercise made me want to wrap my arms around myself and say, "You are safe. You are loved. You are okay. I know this feels very tender, but please don't tuck those uncomfortable feelings away. They hold valuable information that will guide and protect you on your self-reclamation journey."

Developing authenticity isn't an easy process, and it takes time— sometimes even a lifetime. Yet it is worth the effort to commit to the ongoing process of examining the beliefs and behaviors that no longer serve us—or that were not ours to begin with—and replacing them with authentic actions.

Bronnie Ware, a palliative nurse who supported terminally ill patients in their last twelve weeks of life, published *The Top Five Regrets of the Dying.* To help equip you for the Practice in Being Your Authentic Self, consider the third regret from the book: "I wish I hadn't held back my feelings."

Wow, I thought when I came across that statement a few years back. *Holding back our true feelings impacts our life so significantly that it becomes a heavy burden to bear, right down to our very last breath.*

Reading Ware's findings validated my decision to welcome uncomfortable feelings—not just my own, but other people's, too. In a world quick to "power through pain" and "look on the bright side," we so need a healthier response to uncomfortable feelings. We need more people willing say, "All feelings are welcome here. There will be no attempt to fix, dismiss, or cheer you up; I'll just *be* here with you."

One of my most trusted confidants and I inadvertently created a special code for moments when we need to talk through a struggle and hold nothing back.

"I just need to hear your voice," we would text each other when one of us was in despair.

One day I realized what we were actually asking for was someone to hear our true voices—not our fake, forced-optimism voices, but our real, unapologetically honest thoughts, feelings, and words. During those candid conversations, my friend and I would extend empowering permissions to one another. Permissions like:

> When you are in a period of upheaval,
> you are not obligated to create harmony.

> When you encounter a barrier,
> you are not obligated to be open to advice.

> When your back's against the wall,
> you are not obligated to decorate the wall and make it look pretty.

> When you have no words,
> you are not obligated to explain yourself.

> When you know what you need,
> you are not obligated to get prior approval.

> When you are missing pieces,
> you are not obligated to solve the puzzle.

Dear Soul Shift Companion, no matter how you've navigated life up to this point in the journey, today you can choose a new response to feelings of discomfort and pain. This moment marks the end of smiling through gritted teeth and saying everything is "fine" when it's not.

Although we don't always have control over the circumstances that redirect our life, muting our feelings and avoiding the power and vulnerability of an authentic relationship is a choice we get to make. By choosing to embrace our fully human self from this point forward, we can avoid carrying an unnecessary burden and live with more ease.

STEPPING-STONE FOUR
(A PLACE TO STEP OUT)

Dear Soul Shift Companion, it is now time to begin your Practice in Being Your Authentic Self. In this area of exploration, our habit shift is RECONNECTION, which serves as a bridge from *hiding who you are* to *living as you are*.

You may recall that a childhood photo of my uninhibited eight-year-old self and my *Google Island* book helped me remember who I was before the world told me who to be. This led me to discover that reconnecting with our inner child is a very tangible and effective way to begin living more authentically.

Thinking back to who we were, how we behaved, and what we preferred before we were molded by society's expectations and messages can be very enlightening. Childhood ambitions are naturally more authentic because they haven't yet been tainted by external messaging that influences our feelings and actions. Reflecting on experiences that brought us joy as children can remind us to seek the same sense of adventure, spontaneity, and creative freedom in our current lives as adults.

Even if your adult self has forgotten the times when you freely engaged in the delights of your heart without fear of failure or rejection, your inner child still holds those feelings and thoughts. To access these memories for today's practice, please retrieve a childhood photo. Choose a photo of yourself from a time that feels comfortable or from a time you remember well.

Look at your photo and try to remember who you were. Consider things like . . .

What was my favorite television show?

What was my favorite meal?

What place did I like to visit?

Where did I feel safe?

What smells did I like?

How did I prefer to spend my free time?

When did I feel most capable?

One of the most vivid memories from my childhood is that of a long afternoon spent on the swing in my backyard. I swung back and forth for hours, mourning the death of a stray kitten I'd recently adopted. The sun shining on my tear-stained face, the swinging of my shoeless feet, and the weight of my sorrow-filled heart all somehow combined to make me feel seen and accepted, just as I was. Because of that memory, I started visiting swings around my local area as an adult. Whether I was sitting still or in motion, the swing held me in a place of peace and acceptance despite how distressing my world felt at the time.

Dear Soul Shift Companion, it is my hope that what you uncover today will guide you to a place or activity that can offer you this same type of reconnective peace. Before you even think about discouraging yourself by saying you don't remember what you enjoyed doing as a child or where you felt solace, please consider this: you might think that you don't know, but that's only because you haven't allowed yourself the time, space, and permission to listen.

Using the resources that we have in our bodies and the tools we have collected throughout this journey, we are going to explore your memory bank, looking for clues to your authentic self. In this safe space here together, I invite you to call to mind a memory from your younger days. I have provided some possible visualization scenarios to help jog your memory. Read through them slowly. Stop whenever you need to.

Picture yourself in your mind. Perhaps what you see is a bit blurry; maybe you can't see all of the details. That's okay. See yourself when you were competent, curious, excited, engaged. What were you doing?

Visualization 1

Envision yourself exerting your independence. Maybe you are walking to the store by yourself for the first time . . . maybe you are allowed to grab an item in an aisle while your parent is in another part of the store . . . or maybe your teacher has asked you to deliver something to the office.

In these moments of independence, how do you feel? Are you proud? Nervous? Scared? Does being trusted with this task make you feel excited for other activities you might one day do without having to get anyone's permission? Can you remember something you couldn't wait to do on your own?

Visualization 2

Envision yourself creating something with your own two hands. What is it? Maybe it's a fort. Maybe it's a story, or a book. Maybe you're creating something with ingredients from the kitchen. Maybe you're experimenting with spices. Maybe you're making something out of raw materials or dirt and leaves. Whatever you are creating, envision yourself completely engrossed in it. You're delighted by what is developing—not because of the outcome, but by the process. You're in charge. Your ideas are guiding you. You are an artist, a painter, a baker, a woodworker, a problem-solver; you are a creator, and that makes you feel alive.

Visualization 3

Envision yourself in a moment of awe and wonder. Maybe you are witnessing a marching band go by during a parade, your heart beating in time with the big bass drum. Maybe you're holding a kitten or puppy for the first time and you can't fathom how much love you feel for this furry little creature. Maybe you're standing at the shoreline of a vast body of water. The waves of the ocean are lapping up on the shore, and you feel small. Maybe you're thinking, *Wow . . . I wonder what's out there?*

Feel the serenity in your body right now as you reconnect to this familiar place of peace, curiosity, adventure, or joy. Marvel at this little piece of goodness that you found buried under the heaviness of life and the experiences you've had. There's this little seed here, and it just wants you to hold it for a minute and say, "Ah! I remember. Oh yes, I remember!" Just let yourself feel that sense of safety, security, and connection.

Whatever experience came to mind, I want you to recreate a similar situation, space, or activity in the next few days.

Whether it's digging with your hands in the soil, rolling out dough, picking up a paintbrush, walking barefoot in the grass, or wandering the shelves of your local library, be sure to approach it with a *come as you are* mentality. This means that instead of focusing on your appearance, your qualifications, your proficiency, or the outcome of your efforts, your sole focus is your experience. The time spent engaged in creating or relating to your inner child is *yours*, not anybody else's. And the goal of this activity or this practice is connecting with the core of your inner self.

Dear Soul Shift Companion, please set an intention right now to tune into your inner child, your personal guide to the deepest, truest core of who you are. Commit to this intention by writing down the activity you plan to engage in and when:

———————————————————————

Be sure to draw a colorful line or symbol on your living map in the back of the guide after you complete it. Every reconnective experience deepens your pathway to authenticity.

Please grab a sticky note and write down the healing truth that we uncovered today.

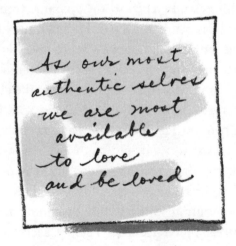

As our most
authentic selves
we are most
available
to love
and be loved

A PEACEFUL SPOT

(a Place to Let Things Sink In)

Stories:

RECONNECT TO CHALLENGE THE LIES

RECONNECT TO KNOW AND BE KNOWN

RECONNECT TO SING YOUR SONG

Reconnect to Challenge the Lies

I always thought I was someone who didn't like to leave her two-mile radius. I always believed I was happier when close to what's familiar. But as I looked through a recent photo album gifted to me by my mom, I realized that was a lie.

As I saw photos of myself in far-off places and remembered the positive feelings I had while walking those uncharted streets and climbing rugged hillsides, I realized an important distinction: **just because I do not like driving outside of my two-mile radius does not mean I am someone who doesn't like to leave her two-mile radius.**

I nearly lived my whole life believing the lie. *Whoa*, I thought. *Imagine if I'd continued to believe this lie—imagine the sights I would've missed and the people I would've never known throughout the remainder of my life.*

As I continued turning the glossy pages, I received another epiphany related to the lies I've believed about myself.

It was a photo of an exquisite house I'd sent to my mom while out on a walk in Arles, France. I'd been walking along the Rhône when I looked up and saw it. My feet promptly stopped walking, as if I'd reached a destination that I wasn't aware I had.

This house spoke to me, and I knew I needed to hear what it had to say. My immediate thought was: *If I could live anywhere, I would*

reside here. This truth struck me. I always thought I was a neighborhood kind of gal with a preference for contemporary homes with
shiny floors, updated cabinets, and manicured walkways. But this
house—the one with the nicks and scratches upon its unique but
comfortingly familiar structure—was ME. I felt so grateful I had the
opportunity to see this particular house so far from anything I knew.
It enabled me to uncover an important truth about where I want to
reside, both literally and figuratively, for the remainder of my life.

I continued flipping through the album, carefully studying the photos Mom had selected to capture the past several years of my life. Each photo seemed to trigger a new truth I'd discovered about myself:

I didn't think I was someone who could feel comfortable speaking in front of a crowd.

I am and I did, leading transformative workshops and feeling very much at home.

I didn't think I was someone who could stand up to a manipulative person.

I am, and it felt freeing to set a healthy boundary for myself without feeling responsible for how it was received.

I didn't think I was someone who could watch my child suffer.

I am, and I will continue to accompany her through a difficult and uncertain time in her life.

I didn't think I was someone who could stop being a people pleaser.

I am, and I have learned to see boundaries as an expression of self-worth and their vital importance for my well-being.

I didn't think I was someone who could read harsh online comments about myself.

I am, and I waste no time reminding myself, "Someone else's opinion is not my truth."

I didn't think I was someone who could sit for hours and work on a jigsaw puzzle.

I am, and I have experienced the wholeness that comes with giving myself time and attention to just *be*.

When I came to the last page of the album, I remembered the disapproving look on a friend's face when, not long before, she told me, "You've changed."

Perhaps that is one way to look at it—or perhaps I am simply discovering who I was all along, before I adopted unauthentic behaviors that I was conditioned to believe made me worthy of love and acceptance.

I flipped back to the beginning of the album wondering if another pass would reveal the point at which I began unraveling these truths. And I believe it began in East Africa—where I took my first, huge step out of my comfort zone, dispelling the notion that I could never journey so far from home.

Like dominoes, once the first lie was exposed, more followed, clearing the way to my true path.

It is so easy to believe we are not someone who can _____ (fill in the blank). Unfortunately, self-doubt can be planted quite early, hindering us before we even have a chance to really discover who we are. Luckily, it is never too late to challenge the lies we've been told or have been telling ourselves and to discover and embrace the truths that align us with our soul.

So, where do we start? We start exactly where we are and take an honest look around. Are we living authentically, or have we gotten comfortable playing a role we were taught to play? We might find we are not truly at home in the life we are living. If so, we must continue our soul-awakening journey by venturing ahead to discover the life we long for. We will likely encounter naysayers along this journey—voices that say things like:

"But why would you want to do that?"

"You aren't capable of that."

"That's not really you, is it?"

And to those people, we will say, "How do you know who I am? I am still figuring it out myself."

Perhaps it will be a house with blue shutters, a red bird on a branch, or a sky full of stars that will stop us in our tracks and offer us a beautiful truth about who we are and why we are here.

Notes to Ponder

I reconnected to my authentic self when I
challenged this belief about myself . . .

Reconnect to Know and Be Known

Hi.
I'm Rachel.
I get lost easily.
I eat popcorn too quickly.
I cry at the drop of a hat.

I feel deeply.
I am a work in progress.
I am honest, but not brutally honest; I think life has enough
"brutal" and does not need more.

When I did my student teaching during college, I was drawn
to the children whose desks were pulled away from the rest.
This led me to become a special education teacher.
I am an encourager.
I am very trusting of people, which is sometimes how I get hurt.

I can be mean when I feel worried or afraid.
Now that I know fear wears disguises, I am compassionate
toward myself when my anxiety spills out.
I am happiest when I am outside walking beneath the trees.
My cat, Banjo, is my ever-present source of peace.

When I was eight years old, I filled notebooks and dreamed of
being an author.
I didn't become a published author until I was thirty-eight.

There was a lot of pain during that thirty-year period, but I am transforming it into purpose.

I believe if we connected more as human beings, our pain would lessen.
Seeing people excluded or alienated pains me more than anything.
I think that's why I try so hard to make people feel seen and accepted.
I think people just want to belong.

I imagine what the world could be if everyone felt like they belonged.
I think the key to belonging is to feel known.
Not only the favorable parts of ourselves but also the tender parts, the vulnerabilities and insecurities.
That's what connects us.

The older I get, the less interested I am in platitudes, surface banter, and glossed-over stories.
I am more interested in what delights your heart, what may have broken it, and what you're doing to heal it.
The pieces of you with the nicks, scratches, and imperfections—that's what I want to know.
Only then do my own complicated pieces start to make a bit more sense.

My name is Rachel.
Each day, I try to show up as my fully human self.
When you see me, you'll know me.
I am the one reaching out my hand to see who reaches back.

Notes to Ponder

I reconnected to my authentic self when I
realized I know this about myself . . .

My "Me" poem might read . . .

Hi. I'm _____. I get _____. I eat _____.
I cry when _____. I feel _____.

I am _____ but not too _____. I get mean when
_____. I feel lost when _____. I am happiest
when _____. You may know me by my_____.

Reconnect to Sing Your Song

I'll never forget the comment that was made on a video I shared of Avery singing a song she wrote to cope with a challenging time in her life. The comment was directed at me, beginning with "Not being an internet troll, I swear . . ."

Comments that start out like that don't usually end well, but curiosity got the best of me, and I kept reading. The commenter went on to state her perception that I write less about Natalie than I do about Avery, and because of that, she feels sad for her.

Comments like that—even when you know they are far from the truth . . . even when you know they come from a place of pain and insecurity . . . even when you know your job is not to appease others—can cause you to pull back your offerings to the world and no longer let people in.

But to hold back an offering in order to avoid being judged, criticized, or misunderstood is a shame. In fact, I'd go as far as to say it's a tragedy.

Here's why:

We all have songs. Every single one of us possesses notes and melodies that, when shared, have the potential to become a comforting anthem for someone else. These songs can come in musical form, like the songs Avery sings, but they can also come in the form of actions, like the ones Natalie creates with flour and butter, seeds and soil.

Each one of us has a song that can better our world. Please don't let the naysayers shut you down. And should they try, please remember these words . . .

> You have a song,
> and I have a song.
> It will take courage to share it.
>
> Because not everyone will understand it.
> Not everyone will be receptive to it.
> Some will find fault in even the most beautiful tune.
> Some will miss the entire anthem because they focus on
> one off-key note.
>
> But this process of offering our songs is not about everyone;
> it's about one—
> that one who needs the very song you wrote.
> That one who feels less alone because of your voice.
> That one who feels brave because she sees her friend
> being brave.
>
> Yes, watching someone sing her song, in her own unique way,
> often inspires others to bravely step forward and sing their
> own songs. Those are some of my favorite kinds of songs.
>
> But when a bottle is thrown at the performer
> the artist
> the creator
> the music maker,

it may cause her to retreat;
to put away her instrument;
to not let another soul hear her song.

If you should witness that tragedy, here's what you should do:

Pick up that bottle and put a flower in it.
Hand it to the human who is being brave
and say, "Keep singing. You have a song someone needs to hear."

Today I'm celebrating us, people who sing their songs,
on stage and in private
online and face-to-face
with instruments and without.
But especially those who feel judged, discouraged, or
misunderstood, wondering if they should hold back their
offering to the world.

In my hand I hold a discarded bottle that was tossed my way.
I think it makes a perfect vase for a flower.

"Keep singing," I say, as I extend this flower to you.

It would be more than a shame—
it would be a downright tragedy
if the world never heard your song.

Notes to Ponder

I reconnected to my authentic self when I heard this song . . .

My "song" is . . .

If I made a playlist of songs that resonate with my
most authentic self, I would include . . .

ASSURANCE FOR YOUR POCKET

May you allow yourself to question what doesn't sit right in your soul.

May you resist the urge to stifle your loudest laugh, your rawest emotion, your deepest need.

May you give your loftiest dreams permission to spread outside the lines.

May you keep taking brave steps to show up as your fully human self, using this truth as the comfiest, most YOU shoes you've ever worn:

I accept who I am right now, in this moment. I will not withhold self-love in anticipation of the person I want to be or the person I hope to become at the end of this journey. I love myself for who I am today, and I will continue to love myself as I learn, grow, and evolve.

PRACTICE SIX
SELF-FORGIVENESS

START HERE . . .

When I was little, I really wanted to see a falling star.

On clear nights, away from the city lights, I'd scan the sky.
Nothing. Nothing to place my wish upon.

I'd forgotten about this childhood longing until recently,
when I stumbled across a collection of fallen stars.
They were scattered next to a trash dumpster.

The sparkly objects had been discarded,
but their radiance could not be diminished or contained.

It crossed my mind that encountering these stars, at that
moment in time, was significant.

There I was, 529 miles from home,
taking my first real walk after recovering from an overuse
injury in my foot,
and what did I see?

I saw stars—
not the iridescent, up-in-the-sky, wished-upon stars,
the crinkled, down-in-the-dirt, all-used-up stars.

They pulled me in.
And when I bent down to investigate,
the flittering, metallic paper caught the light of the sun.

Maybe it was my fading eyesight,
the worry lines around my eyes,
or the salt of too many tears,
but I felt very, very lucky to see these stars.

These are *Worthy of Wishes* stars, I decided . . .

Tested but not terminated
jaded but not permanently jinxed
vacated but not without value.

As much as I wanted to pick up one of those worthy stars and
carry it with me,
I didn't.

I left it for the next traveler who came to that point in their
journey—
the point when they realize life is too precious to hold our
Worthy Wishes for celestial stars.

Release them now,
on handwritten apology notes,
rusty old pennies tossed in whatever form of fountain you
can find,
and through jumbled words of bedtime prayers.

These wishes may not ride on stars with long, glowing tails,
but they carry remarkable strength still.

Recognize your worthiness in these stars—and let them pull
you in.
Your radiance cannot be diminished or contained.

typically don't like to spoil a good surprise, but in this case, I am overjoyed to tell you what's ahead in the Soul Shift journey. It is this liberating truth: *Today matters more than yesterday. Your story is still being written.*

Feel these words, will you? Breathe them in.

Today matters more than yesterday. Your story is still being written.

Does that statement make you breathe easier? Feel lighter? More hopeful?

And if you can't fathom the thought, will you simply consider it? Will you consider that the choices you make today hold the greatest possibility of any moment in time?

Thank you for saying yes. By doing so, you have already removed one obstacle from your path of self-forgiveness.

Let me explain . . .

Today holds great hope, but there is one condition: you must get out of your own way.

When it comes to the Practice of Self-Forgiveness, we, ourselves, are the biggest obstacles we'll encounter. But if we are willing to learn how to set down our unhealthy baggage—which includes the mistakes, missed opportunities, and regrets we carry—we can move past these obstacles. That means we can travel lighter and freer through the rest of our days on a path that aligns our gifts with the needs of the world.

I don't know about you, but the idea of traveling with greater ease in a purposeful direction makes me eager to get started. We still have a patch of hindering overgrowth ahead of us, but as promised, we are going to clear a path together. With each of the following new reflections I share, I hope you'll be reminded that the Soul Shift journey is not a linear path; it winds, dips, and bends. And with each brave step, there is a chance you'll encounter pain, but as I can attest, those points of discomfort offer valuable awareness. With awareness comes the opportunity to let go of long-standing regrets so you can focus on what you *can* control: your choices in the present day. That is where possibility thrives.

Let's get started . . .

The experience that sparked my Practice of Self-Forgiveness happened a little over a decade ago. I was sitting in a church service in my new community. At the time, there weren't a lot of places where I felt like I could breathe. But this church, with its inclusive practices and diverse community of members, offered a haven. For the first time in my adult life, I'd found a church home where there was a seat for everyone at the table.

And because of that, I arrived every Sunday with a mindset of acceptance not only for others, but also for myself.

That morning, the pastor was talking about forgiveness. At the conclusion of his message, small pieces of paper were passed out. The congregation was told we could write down the name of someone we wanted to forgive.

I didn't even need to think about it.

Me. I want to forgive myself.

Just that morning, I'd ruminated over misplacing my car keys and being gruff with my family as we left the house. On top of that, I'd been growing more and more aware of the damaging impact my past choices and behavior had on my current relationships.

Reflecting on the pain I'd inflicted brought feelings of shame and regret, which consequently created an obstacle. I felt I was at a crossroads, unsure of how to proceed in my journey given there was a great deal of heaviness to carry.

I felt both deep pain and immense relief while staring at the word "MYSELF" written on that piece of paper. It was while I was in this complicated emotional space that my painful truth became clear:

Until I can forgive myself for the mistakes of the past, I can't truly live and fully love.

Judgment for past failures was a self-imposed obstacle hindering me from grasping the joy in the present moment. Continuing to serve as my personal judge and jury would sabotage my ability to show up in the moment and for future opportunities.

Since posting visual reminders throughout my house was helping reinforce my other Soul Shift practices, I decided to write a self-forgiveness intention and post it on my mirror where I could recite it each day. When I got home from church, I wrote this on a sticky note: "Today I release myself from the role of Judge. When I inflict self-judgment, I am unable to love myself, nurture my family, or share my gifts with the world."

I remember wondering why I specifically chose self-judgment as my starting point. I think "forgiving myself" just felt far too vague and overwhelming while considering how to stop "judging myself" felt like a measurable step. I soon understood the connection: when we beat ourselves up over mistakes or second-guess something we did, we are judging ourselves. And when we stand in judgment of ourselves, we prevent ourselves from moving forward and making a different choice in the here and now.

Notice I said "choice." I cannot emphasize how important that piece is.

When my pastor asked, "Who do you want to forgive?" and I wrote "myself," that was monumental; it was the first time I realized: *I have a choice. I can remain in judgment of myself, or I can choose to set down my baggage and live.*

Recognizing that I could choose to forgive myself gave strength to my stride. *I want to forgive myself, but how?* I decided to start by facing the regret that bubbled to the surface most frequently: inflicting emotional distress on my first-born child, Natalie.

Since writing was my most comfortable form of communication, I decided to write Natalie a note that I would read to her at bedtime.

The note began with the many things I loved about her eight-year-old self—the way she thought about people who were suffering and took active steps to help them . . . the way she gave everything her all, whether it was swimming in a race or making a cake . . . the way she set personal goals and took initiative to achieve them.

The second part of the note was an apology, which never came easy for me. I encouraged myself to not overthink it, to just be honest and say what she deserved to hear:

> I'm sorry I don't always take the time to tell you all the things I love about you.

> I'm sorry I tend to point out the things you could improve on instead of taking time to acknowledge the million things you do right.

I'm sorry that I have made you feel responsible for my emotions, especially my angry ones.

I'm sorry for the expectations I have put on you that were not reasonable, fair, or appropriate.

I am working on learning to love myself so I can love you better, in the ways you deserve to be loved. I know my actions have hurt you, and I hope, in time, you can see the changes I am making and can forgive me.

When I read the note to Natalie at bedtime, she seemed a bit surprised but interested in what I was saying. When I was finished, Natalie leaned over and hugged me for the longest time. I felt a tremendous weight lift from my body. From that point on, apologetic words flowed more readily from my lips. I realized mistakes were not something to be ashamed of and avoided at all costs. With every misstep and willingness to acknowledge it, there was opportunity for growth, connection, and compassion.

As my children grew and began making mistakes with bigger consequences, I was grateful I'd been modeling the notion that just because you fail at something doesn't mean you *are* a failure. Seeing me openly acknowledge and work through my mistakes allowed my kids to view me as a trusted source of support when something went astray in their lives. My kids were willing to share their humanness with me because I had chosen to be transparent with them. From there, a new healing truth emerged: **the mistakes of yesterday are stepping-stones to the lovingly imperfect, grace-filled person I am today.**

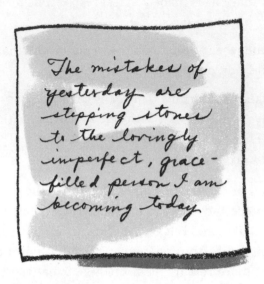

The mistakes of yesterday are stepping stones to the lovingly imperfect, grace-filled person I am becoming today

Dear Soul Shift Companion, would you like to start seeing your mistakes as stepping-stones and using them to move forward? Although we can't undo the damage that's been done, we CAN embrace the possibilities of today. With awareness and compassion, it's possible to heal our fractured reflections about the past and create a clear vision of hope for the present and the future, for you and for the ones you love.

Let's keep going . . .

STEPPING-STONE ONE
(A PLACE TO JUST BE)

Before we can truly set down our baggage, we must prepare by having realistic expectations about this process. Yes, *process.* Self-forgiveness is not a one-time effort; it's an ongoing practice. As shame, regret, or pain come up from past mistakes, no matter how recent or long ago they occurred, the key is to choose **not** to push the pain away but instead to acknowledge it. By choosing to reflect on the situation with curiosity and compassion, you are better able to understand what might have influenced your choices at the time of the misstep.

Not only have I gained compassion for my past self by repeating the self-forgiveness process, I have also discovered the four components needed for me to experience full and complete release. Each time I truly want to set down baggage, I know I must:

1. Acknowledge my mistake
2. Apologize if my mistake or behavior impacted someone else
3. Compassionately consider why I may have made that poor choice or behaved that way
4. Consider how I am using the experience to grow or enhance my life or the life of someone else

My self-forgiveness process does not always go in that order or appear so clear and concise, but setting the expectation that this is a practice that requires patience, compassion, and grace has helped me face some of my most painful regrets that have haunted me for many years.

One major baggage release came after a holiday visit with Scott's extended family. I noticed that every time we got together, a painful vacation memory would surface, and I'd feel deeply ashamed. I decided this would be the last time I would push it away; I would sit with it and hopefully release it once and for all.

The memory, or more like a collection of memories, happened during a weeklong beach visit with a large group of family members. Around that time, I'd experienced several major life stressors, including an out-of-state move and the birth of my second child. During that trip, I was angry, short-tempered, distant, and abrupt to everyone around me. On one occasion, the suggestion of extending my baby's bedtime to accommodate our large party at a restaurant resulted in me squealing my tires as I left the parking lot. Thinking about my behavior, even a decade later, made my face burn with shame.

But how long must I punish myself for doing the very best I could at the time, given the emotional state I was in? My actions, although undesirable, came from a basic human survival instinct. I did not deserve to punish myself any longer for the limited awareness I had and the poor choices I made because of it.

So, more than ten years after that painful week, I sent my mother-in-law the following text: "Hi Patti. You know that trip to Orange Beach when the girls were little? I feel really sad when I think about how I behaved, and I am very sorry for the pain I caused. Thank you for loving me when I was so hard to love."

Since my mother-in-law and I text often, I expected she'd respond pretty quickly. Little did I know she was out to lunch with a girlfriend and would not look at her phone for several hours.

In that waiting period, I had to ask myself a hard question: *What if Patti doesn't forgive me?*

That was when I reminded myself, *I didn't apologize solely to receive her forgiveness; I apologized to offer myself forgiveness—to set down my baggage.*

A few hours later, Patti responded with love and understanding, adding that every single one of us has behaved in ways we are not proud of when we are in a place of pain and struggle.

But what if she had not responded with such grace? I believe I would have still felt a sense of peace knowing I took responsibility for my actions and addressed my wrongdoing.

And honestly, that was all I *could* do. But one thing still bothered me: Why did it take me so long to apologize?

One of my Soul Shift participants shed light on this, expanding on the notion that self-forgiveness is a process, not a switch to click on and off. She wrote:

> As I've pondered your self-forgiveness message, I've become aware of the fact that we are unable to receive our own love and forgiveness if we have not done the work to become our authentic selves. These two concepts, living authentically and letting go of past mistakes, are actually building blocks; only then can you add on your practice of self-worth as another building block.
>
> We cannot risk becoming authentic and release the baggage if we do not consider ourselves worthy of the opportunity right in front of us. We can hug others, but

we cannot fully feel it until we believe we are worthy of the hug.

We can hear "I Love You," but we cannot truly accept it unless we believe we have a right to this love. We can receive, "I forgive you," but we cannot fully embrace it if we do not believe it is ours to hold.

As my Soul Shift Companion helped me understand, the foundation of self-forgiveness was laid through my Practice of Presence, which taught me that I am worthy of showing up for every moment of my life. Subsequent practices, like the Practice of True Self-Worth, helped me embrace true self-forgiveness, which is not dependent on another person's response.

Dear Soul Shift Companion, would you like to take a significant step toward making this shift? What's ahead will offer you a chance to make peace within—perhaps like never before—so you can focus your energy on taking healthy actions today and in the future.

STEPPING-STONE TWO
(A PLACE TO BECOME AWARE)

Dear Soul Shift Companion, it is time to begin shifting our focus from shame and anguish for past behaviors and regretful choices and start uncovering pathways that can help you get back on track, even after missteps along the way. That is the purpose of this self-reflective exercise. The following check-in questions are designed to help you search within yourself for the most direct route to self-forgiveness on your personal journey. Even one small insight can offer the perspective you need to view the horizon ahead through a more positive and capable lens.

1. In your own words, what does self-forgiveness mean to you?

2. Does self-forgiveness come easily to you, or do you find it difficult? Why do you think that is?

3. Are there certain past mistakes that you continually relive? Is there anything you can do to rectify those mistakes now? If not, what might you say to yourself about the lessons learned from those mistakes as a way of offering yourself grace?

4. What would you most like to forgive yourself for? What impact do you think the release of that unhealthy baggage would have on your life or your relationships?

STEPPING-STONE THREE
(A PLACE TO PREPARE THE WAY)

Dear Soul Shift Companion, the best way to fortify ourselves for the lifelong Practice of Self-Forgiveness is by garnering a steady supply of self-compassion. I have found that a very effective way to tap into self-compassion is by speaking to my inner child or my younger self. The following exercise offers you a chance to do that with steady support from me.

In the space below, write yourself a forgiveness note. This may include: 1) identifying your past actions that have hurt you or someone you love, 2) identifying what you have learned or how you have grown from the mistake, and/or 3) identifying a relevant self-forgiveness affirmation.

Before you begin, let me walk you through the process using a note I wrote to myself:

Dear Precious Self,

Your harsh reactions and scary outbursts when your children were young were not because you were a mean person or a bad mom; they were symptoms of the unmet needs inside of you. They were your cry for help, your way of saying, "Something is not working here, and I need help to fix it."

Looking at the stressful circumstances you faced and the emotional state you were in, I can see you were doing the best you could with the tools you had at the time.

I am proud of the ways you are using your past regrets in this area to more effectively communicate your needs and feelings in the present day. Do you realize that when you get frustrated, anxious, or irritated, you no longer lash out? You pay attention to the signals your body gives you, and you've learned to apply healthy coping mechanisms, ask for help, or express your needs. Recently, you expressed some difficult things very well. You said, "I feel unappreciated when . . ." and "I feel insecure when . . ." and "I feel fragile right now, so I am going to need . . ."

By learning to respond compassionately to your inner child when she is tired, anxious, overwhelmed, scared, or depressed, you are essentially reparenting yourself. By connecting to your inner child with assurance, care, and grace, you are learning to compassionately respond to your kids when they are anxious, overwhelmed, scared, or depressed. What an incredible gift!

With this understanding, I commend you for using your regrets as stepping-stones to become the compassionate and grace-filled parent and human being you are today. Please forgive yourself. It is time.

Love,

Rachel

Dear Soul Shift Companion, when you are ready, your note can be written here (or on a separate piece of paper if you prefer).

Dear Precious Self,

I know it's been difficult to forgive you for . . .

But looking back at the situation with compassion and curiosity, I see that at the time you were . . .

I've noticed that you are trying to do things differently now by . . .

Using what you have learned from this regretful experience, there are benefits like . . .

With this understanding, I commend you for using painful experiences as a stepping-stone to become . . .

Please set the baggage down now. Please forgive yourself.
It is time.

Your name

If you feel protective of what you have written, please remember, this is your self-forgiveness note to do with as you wish. Equipping yourself to be more self-compassionate does not come so much from the physical document as it does from the process of walking through this exercise. And the beauty of this tool is that you can use it any time feelings of shame or regret come up. The option of writing a forgiveness note to your inner child or past self is always available when you need a healthy dose of self-compassion and grace.

STEPPING-STONE FOUR
(A PLACE TO STEP OUT)

Dear Soul Shift Companion, now that we have covered some vital areas around self-judgment, past mistakes, and meeting ourselves with compassion, it is time to begin our Practice of Self-Forgiveness. In this area of exploration, our habit shift is RELEASE, which serves as the bridge from "I can't truly live and love until I forgive myself" to a new, healing truth: "My mistakes were stepping-stones to the person I am becoming today."

We can get some serious momentum on our path to self-forgiveness by implementing three practical tools I like to call "baggage releasers." Instead of holding regret and carrying it for days and years, we can release it almost immediately using any of these practical methods.

Remember, it's small steps—not massive leaps—that create the positive and lasting transformation you are seeking. A Practice of Self-Forgiveness is not a one-time effort; it's an ongoing process that will serve you well for the rest of your life. These three actionable, daily release rituals can be very effective in nurturing that process.

Baggage Releaser #1: Role Release

As I became aware of my critical inner voice through my Practice in Being Kind to Yourself, I began to recognize when my inner judge was in control. It said things like:

"I can't believe you did that."

"You're failing."

"You're a bad mom/partner/daughter/friend."

In addition to using my "only love today" phrase to redirect my inner bully, I also started extending compassion to my inner judge.

I would say things like, "I hear you, Judge. I know you're showing up because you're trying to protect me from getting hurt or rejected, but I know now that I can trust the guidance of my soul; it's indicating I need to show up right now. I may make a mistake, but that's part of living and trying. So, thank you, Judge, you can sit down now. I got this."

Over time, I noticed some profound results from releasing my inner judge from her role. I was better able to grasp the precious moment at hand, take more risks, try new things, connect more authentically, and extend compassion toward myself when I messed up.

If you are well acquainted with your inner judge and the impact this voice has on you, I have some really good news: You don't have to continue to fill that role. You can let that job go.

Take a moment right now to compassionately dismiss your inner judge:

Baggage Releaser #2: Ritual Release

I started the release ritual I am about to describe when my daughters were young, yet it is one they occasionally still ask for even in their teen years. We call it "the heartbeat check": I visit them one-on-one before bedtime, ask them if I can place my head on their chest, and then proceed to tell them what I hear. While one daughter's heartbeat check commonly brings laughter, my other daughter's heartbeat check often leads to a philosophical discussion. Yet, in both instances, there is one commonality: the heartbeat check offers a chance to make peace. No matter what we have said or done that day to disappoint ourselves or each other, listening to the human heart helps us focus on what is important, sometimes without even using words.

The heartbeat check is just one example of a practice that helps us let go of mistakes, make amends, and live in the moment. I hope this inspires you to discover your own connective and liberating ritual.

Take a moment and describe a daily release ritual you have in place or would like to establish.

This could be a solitary activity like tending/talking to your plants, lighting a special candle, or standing with your face toward the sun and imagining the heaviness you carry slowly melting away. Your release ritual could also include companions or family members by initiating a three-minute dance party to reset a bad morning, sharing a high/low of the day, or offering a blank piece of paper and saying, "Your story isn't over; it is still being written. What would you like the next page to say?" Go ahead and try this baggage releaser for yourself right now:

Baggage Releaser #3: Recollection Release

This practice requires you to think about a time when you felt most forgiven. What did it sound like, smell like, look like, taste like? To spark your memory, I'd like to share a recollection that never fails to help me meet my mistakes with compassion . . .

When I was about four years old, my parents took my sister and me to the home of family friends. They did not have children, so I felt it was important to be extra grown-up and polite.

After dinner, we got to create our own serving of strawberry shortcake. No one said a word as I piled on the strawberries and mounds of whipped cream. As I was walking out to their screened-in porch to enjoy my dessert, I tripped and fell. My delicious masterpiece flew across the floor, hitting the walls and making a sticky disaster.

When the couple came rushing out to the porch to see what had happened, I blurted, "I'm sorry I made such a mess."

And I'll never forget what the woman said: "Never mind the mess . . . are YOU okay? That's what I want to know. Are YOU okay?"

Her response to my mistake surprised me, calmed me, and made me feel more than okay.

When the couple returned with a freshly made dessert, I remember how good it tasted—not just because the strawberries were from the garden and the cake was from scratch. No, it was because of the grace they extended.

My well-being was more important than the mess.

That really hit the spot.

I keep that recollection close to my heart for times when I feel like I made a mess of things. Instead of prioritizing the mistake, I try to focus on my well-being.

How is my heart?

How is my spirit?

How is my soul?

Instead of burdening myself with feelings of annoyance, guilt, or shame, focusing on well-being (like my parents' friend did for me) helps me extend grace and compassion. Those types of responses are what encourage humans to get back up and keep reaching for life's fruitful moments.

Describe a moment in your life when you felt truly forgiven (include scent, taste, sound, and feeling):

Beloved Soul Shift Companion, you now possess three readily available baggage releasers that can extend healing forgiveness far beyond yourself. Which releaser resonated with you the most? Commit to implementing this practice by writing down your intention:

Be sure to draw a colorful line or symbol on your living map in the back of the guide after implementing it. With every baggage-releasing experience, you are a little lighter, a little freer to move, breathe, live, and love. Your remarkable self, made of every stumble and misstep you've ever made, is needed in this world.

Please grab a sticky note and write down the healing truth that we uncovered today.

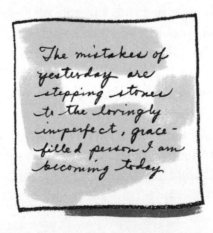

The mistakes of yesterday are stepping stones to the lovingly imperfect, grace-filled person I am becoming today

A PEACEFUL SPOT

(a Place to Let Things Sink In)

Stories:

RELEASE TO SEIZE THE OPPORTUNITIES OF TODAY

RELEASE TO KICK SHAME TO THE CURB

RELEASE TO SALVAGE WHAT'S BEEN RUINED

Release to Seize the Opportunities of Today

Taking our biennial beach trip with Scott's family means getting to spend quality time with my young niece and nephews. It doesn't seem to matter what age they are when the trip rolls around; feelings of regret tend to creep up due to its association with the vacation where I behaved so badly. But I've learned to combat those sabotaging thoughts by showing up in ways I wish I had when my kids were young.

For one particular weeklong trip, I filled an entire backpack with carefully selected picture books from my daughters' childhood collection.

Each night, I laid out all the books and let the kids choose two for me to read. The four of us would pile into one bed and cuddle up close. I used my best character voices. I stopped to answer questions. I did not rush. My internal mantra was: "Be here now."

The ability to be present is not something that comes naturally to me. It is something I've learned how to do and must continually practice. But the effort has paid off; not only do I get to experience life as it is happening, but I also get to experience connection with the people I love. By recognizing that it is unreasonable to judge myself for what I wasn't able to do in the past, I am able to completely lean into these connective moments. Being there physically, mentally, *and* emotionally creates opportunities to build love and trust, no matter how much or little time we have together.

Despite my belief that today matters more than yesterday, I felt unreasonably sad when that weeklong reading ritual ended.

"I'm going to miss reading to you," I said to my nephew, Sam, on that last day.

"Don't be sad, Aunt Rachel," Sam said. But I couldn't seem to shake the feeling that my chances to experience cozy moments huddled under a blanket with my kids were all used up. After all, I was heading home with teenagers who fell asleep to white noise and LED lights, not Mom narrating their favorite bedtime story.

Later that night, with a half-unpacked suitcase strewn across her bedroom floor, Avery began her bedtime preparations. From her unmade bed, I quietly observed as she completed a face-washing routine that lasted longer than mine; I listened as she lingered over what to write on the tiny note inside her prayer box; I reached out as she struggled with her back brace and asked for help.

> Through it all,
> I was patient.
> I was compassionate.
> I was funny.
> I was encouraging.
> I was present.

I wasn't reading my daughter picture books anymore, but I was right there in the current chapter of her life, showing up in the moment that mattered.

That's when it hit me. My chances to be present were not all used up; they might not look the same as they did before, but they were still there. The key was to stop punishing myself long enough to see them.

Can you see them, too?

With a compassionate and intentional mindset, the possibilities of today expand exponentially. Here are some ideas for reframing your mindset to capitalize on the chances that exist today:

> Over time, you've learned to love without conditions . . . who might need your newfound way of loving today?

Over time, you've learned to be more patient . . . who might need to experience your new willingness to wait now?

Over time, you've found your soothing voice . . . who might need to hear unexpected gentleness in your tone today?

Over time, you've learned to let down your walls . . . who might need to be drawn closer to the real you today?

Beyond the mistakes, regrets, and could-have-beens, there are second, third, and forty-seventh chances.
Seize them.
It's not too late.
Today matters more than yesterday.

Notes to Ponder

I released baggage by choosing to turn a
regret into a second chance by . . .

Release to Kick Shame to the Curb
(Content warning: sexual assault*)

I'm done sabotaging my health.
I'm done shaming my body.
I've been connecting dots, and it's allowed me to love myself
more wholly than ever before.

What happened my sophomore year was not my fault.
This empowering statement changes everything.
It changes the way I see my body that is worthy of loving
regard and care.
Perhaps there's not enough water in the world to quench my
parched soul, but I can start with one glass.
I will start today.

Some would call it a "health kick."
I've called it that many times before as I attempted to consume
less sugar, less processed foods, and less diet soda.
But it never lasted long; I always sabotaged myself.
Enough diet soda to die a slow death, I joked.
If only it had been a joke.
I'd been sabotaging my body, withholding good things from it,
because of shame.
I see the connection now.

So, I'm not calling this a "health kick." This is a "shame kick."
It's twenty-some years long overdue, but it's not too late—
I refuse to die a slow death.

I've never been an emotional eater, but on this particular day,
I sat in a vacation rental stuffing my mouth while "breaking
news" flashed upon the TV screen.

I'd never considered what happened my sophomore year as a
violation.
In my mind, it was
my mistake,
my misjudgment,
my poor choice—as if one could make purple bruises in
intimate places on her own body.

When I woke up, my dress was missing beads.
And I blamed myself.
For twenty-seven years, I blamed myself and what I wore, the
alcohol I drank, and the trust I naively gave my date.

But sitting there, decades later, listening to a woman's
powerful testimony on national news, I realized it wasn't
my fault.

Tearfully, I looked down at my body, particularly my stomach—a place I forbade anyone to touch. I saw how it all connected to that night.

When I told a trusted friend what I remembered, there was dead silence. I held my breath as she gathered the courage to speak her truth, thirty-two years long overdue.

"Me too, Rach . . . me too."

As we held each other, I felt this rare sense of hope:

Do you think this could be the beginning of us loving ourselves wholly—
instead of conditionally,
sporadically,
and incompletely?

My dot connected to her dot, and together we were able to form a new picture of wholeness we couldn't grasp before. Our "shame kick" began the minute we grasped the truth.

We are worthy of a shame-free existence.
We are worthy of moving our bodies freely.
We are worthy of loving respect.
We are worthy of nutrient-rich food.
We are worthy of water for our parched souls.
There may not be enough water in the world to quench this thirst, but we can start with one glass.

Let's start by placing the shame where it belongs:
Not on us.
Not for one more day.

We are worthy.
We are not alone.
I see the connection now.

*RAINN is a confidential sexual assault hotline: 1-800-656-4673

Notes to Ponder

I released baggage when I noticed I was engaging
in a body-shaming behavior and I . . .

Release to Salvage What's Been Ruined

I'll never forget when Avery's guitar instructor challenged her to write one new song per month. At the end of every month, they would share their songs with each other.

Avery's complaint about this challenge was pretty valid. She said, "I don't have as many life experiences as Mr. Corey. I mean . . . he's been in love! That's pretty much what all the good songs are about!"

We laughed, not knowing that in the months and years ahead, she would be provided with songwriting material one might never wish to have. Pain, challenge, struggle, and uncertainty will provide loads of inspiration if you allow them to.

The best way to describe that period was *ruined* . . . plans ruined . . . dreams ruined . . . normal childhood ruined. "This is not how it is supposed to be," she often said.

When Avery's album came out, people made a big deal about it. "What a go-getter," they said. But the truth was, Avery didn't set out to record an album; she went to her place of peace to cope with life's challenges, and what came forth was music with universal themes of human struggle.

People who were close to our family knew the painful inspiration behind the songs. One day, a family friend tagged me in an Instagram post with the comment "For Avery . . ." I looked at the featured image, instantly recognizing the calligraphic style of the Boy and the Mole, characters from Charlie Mackesy's book, *The Boy, the Mole, the Fox and the Horse*. In the drawing, the characters were sitting across from each other. Between them, a scrap of a music score peeked through a rip in the paper. Around the characters were these words written in bold, black ink:

"Is it ruined?"
  "No," said the mole, "look at the music, it often comes through where things are broken."

—Charlie Mackesy

As tears flooded my eyes, I ran upstairs to my bedroom where the book *The Boy, the Mole, the Fox, and the Horse* sat. *How could I have missed this page?* I wondered, quickly flipping through each page to find the one with the music.

After going through the book three times, I realized that page, that message, was not in the book. It had been created for social media for this very moment, when it's so tempting to look at our upended lives with the stains, spills, rips, cancellations, derailments, and disappointments and think to ourselves: IT IS RUINED. It's all ruined . . .

And in our darkest moments, as I can attest, we might even be tempted to say, "I am ruined. I am all ruined."

But in the fragile moments, something comes through the brokenness . . .

It's a song.
It's a promise.
It's an understanding.
It's an answer.
It's a step.
It's an awakening.

Listen.
Look.
See.

BELIEVE.
It is not ruined.
YOU are not ruined.
You are courageous and brave, and you are here, despite all the ways life has tried to derail you.

As you seek to ease your own pain, you may ease the pain of someone else.

"Where did these lyrics come from?" the grateful recipient will one day say.

And we will remember this moment, when you made the brave choice to see what can be salvaged after the storm.

Notes to Ponder

I released baggage when I realized something I
thought was ruined actually wasn't because . . .

ASSURANCE FOR YOUR POCKET

May you assure yourself of these truths so often that they become known by heart:

I did the best I could, given what I knew at the time.

I am worthy of forgiveness. No one needs to hold onto such a burden for so long.

I can do everything "right" and things can still go horribly wrong.

I forgive myself for expecting me to know what I didn't know.

I will stop wounding myself for things I cannot change, so I can start healing the life that is here to live now.

May the baggage you set down allow you to stand taller and see possibility on the horizon with this liberating truth:

Shame is not a healthy motivator because it dismisses the unseen pain beneath the brave effort it took to show up. I am here now. That is what matters.

PRACTICE SEVEN
LOOKING AFTER YOURSELF

To the Barely Breathing Doers
the Worn-Out Worriers
the Can't-Take-Another-Step Supporters
the I-Could-Use-Some-Help Helpers
. . . *permission to pause.*

When life feels overwhelming,
it's easy to believe that if you can't keep up,
then you should drop out of the race.

Don't believe the lie.

You have options that our breakneck world doesn't want you
to know about,
so, I'll tell you.
They are called LIFE'S LITTLE VICTORIES . . .

Don't drop out of the race today;
just stop focusing on the finish line.
Notice the sidewalk cracks that hold a flower,
reach for the person running next to you and say,
"Let's take a breather."
Don't drop out of the race,
just rest on the curb and catch your breath.

Sit and cheer for the workers, helpers, holders,
and supporters you see going by,
and give your blisters time to heal.

Don't drop out of the race,
just remember there is more than one route,
and this is not about big wins or shiny trophies—
it's about collecting quiet triumphs along the way.
Those moments we feel connected to fellow humans,
Mother Nature,
our very own hearts.

In case no one ever told you:
who you are becoming is far more important
than where you are going.

So, please, don't drop out of the race today.
Collect one of life's little victories.

When you get back up, you may find you aren't behind;
you are ahead,
winning by living
one sacred breath at a time.

spent quite a bit of time thinking about what to call this practice area. Out of the eight territories along your Soul Shift journey, this one has the potential to make the greatest impact on your quality of life. I considered calling it a Practice in Self-Care, which would have been appropriate, but given how the term "self-care" has become a trendy buzzword, I decided against it. The last thing I wanted was for you to view this practice as a luxurious afterthought, something you *treat* yourself to after you've reached a goal, checked all the boxes, or collapsed from exhaustion. I wanted you to see this practice as a routine, consistent, and prioritized investment in your health and well-being.

Why is this practice worthy of such prioritization? Because a well-cared-for state of being positively impacts every aspect of your life—and it has the potential to impact the world. In the book *Where to Begin*, activist and poet Cleo Wade writes, "Self-care is how we claim peace of mind. When we know how to gift peace to our inner world, the pathway to creating peace in the world around us is so much clearer."

I am drawn to Cleo Wade's notion that peace gifted to our inner world creates peace in our outer world. It sounds really beautiful, doesn't it? But if we're being realistic, we know that caring for our inner selves is much easier said than done.

The question I continually find myself asking is, *How?* How are human beings supposed to find the time, energy, and space to honor our deepest needs when it's difficult to meet even the most basic ones?

I think it begins by changing our perception of this vital practice, which is another reason I opted *not* to call it A Practice in Self-Care and instead chose a Practice in Looking After Yourself. "Self-care" sounds vague and consumerist; "look after" is practical and direct. We know exactly what it means to look after someone or something because we do it all the time. Whether it's making sure our loved ones are nourished, rested, equipped, informed, or supported, we look after them, time after time.

But when it comes to us looking after ourselves . . . well, this is where it gets tricky—and through no fault of our own. From a young age, women are conditioned to put others first and as a result carry enormous amounts of mental, physical, and emotional labor. Over time, the stress builds up, wreaking havoc on our health and well-being.

Although the idea of shifting the balance from constantly pouring *from* ourselves to routinely investing *in* ourselves may feel impossible, uncomfortable, or even self-indulgent, our very lives depend on making this shift. The practice area ahead is designed to help you feel equipped and supported as you make that critical shift. The stories and exercises you'll find here are designed to help you begin recognizing the relationship you have with yourself, prioritizing it, and putting forth intentional effort to give yourself the same care you give others.

Let's get started . . .

My practice of looking after myself was sparked by a medical emergency I never saw coming. It wasn't pretty and it's not easy to share, but I choose to be transparent in hopes of helping someone else avoid a similar outcome.

I'd just finished writing the manuscript for my second book. In order to meet my publisher's deadline, I'd deprived myself of sleep, movement, and nourishment. To make matters worse, I'd adapted to a nearly constant physical ache. For months, I'd simply thrown antibiotics at what seemed to be a never-ending bladder infection because I didn't have the bandwidth to have it properly assessed. As a result, everything came crashing down (literally) in a moment of frustration after dinner one evening.

In an unexpected fit of rage, I raised a glass casserole dish above my head and smashed it down on the kitchen counter. Natalie, who was twelve at the time, happened to be rinsing off her dinner dish. Needless to say, my outburst frightened her. It scared me, too, but not for the same reason. Shocked and ashamed, I wondered how someone who had just written a book on prioritizing the moments that matter had let herself get to this point.

After collecting myself, I went to Natalie's room to apologize. I found her sitting on her bed looking worried and scared.

"I am so sorry. I did not handle my frustration well at all," I said to her. "And I think it's because I'm not taking good care of myself."

In response to my confession, I received a very unexpected reaction. Natalie's face lit up as her eyes shifted to the stack of medical textbooks my mom had bought at a garage sale. Apparently, Natalie had been studying them and was just waiting for the opportunity to share some life-enhancing tips.

"Mom, you really need to get at least seven hours of sleep each night. And it's important to get your heart rate up when you exercise. You definitely need to drink more water and cut back on all the diet sodas. I can make you some delicious iced tea, Mom . . . peach, blueberry, pomegranate . . . anything you want."

Three things immediately struck me about Natalie's response to my confession: 1) she was clearly concerned about the way I was existing, 2) her ideas were small and practical, similar to the strategies I was using to cultivate my other practices, and 3) she was expressing her love for me through caretaking solutions.

Natalie's response seemed to put words to the nagging feeling I'd been pushing aside for months, which was: *You need to take care of yourself!*

Within days, I provided myself with accountability by announcing three goals from Natalie's list of suggestions that I was going to try to do each day. The goals were: get seven hours of sleep, drink less diet soda, and consume more water. I told my family specifically how I was going to try to follow through and how they could help support my endeavors.

I also made a medical appointment to get to the bottom of the six-months-long bladder infection. This was where the big awakening occurred.

After going to a series of doctors, a highly experienced urologist discovered a monster-sized kidney stone that was taking up over half of my kidney. Left unattended, this condition could have been life-altering. However, when the doctor described a very archaic and painful process for removal, I decided to get a second opinion.

When I relayed the information to the second urologist, she gasped and said, "You could have lost a year of your life due to complications from the wrong procedure."

But do you know what I heard?

"You could have lost your life."

And not just from the improper removal of a giant kidney stone, but from not looking after myself in the first place.

And there it was—my painful truth.

With full clarity, I realized, **I am not invincible, and if I don't start investing in my health and well-being, I will lose (at least some of) my life.**

This brutal wake-up call pushed me to do whatever was needed to get rid of the blockage. The extraction process ended up requiring two hospital stays and months of treatment from complications that arose.

Almost a year after the kidney stone discovery, I stood in my doctor's office finally hearing these long-awaited words: "You don't need to make another appointment. Hopefully, we won't see you for a while."

With my internal pain slowly subsiding, my elevated blood pressure back to normal, and my pristine blood work, I was free to go on with my life.

It wasn't until I pushed the elevator button—the one I'd pushed with shaky hands over and over throughout the long, painful period—that I was overcome with emotion.

"I won't be back here for a long, long time," I whispered, both as a promise and a prayer.

And when I caught my reflection in the elevator doors, I saw someone I love very much . . . ME.

From that reflection, a new, healing truth surfaced:

I love myself enough to take care of all of me—body, mind, spirit, and soul.

I learned to approach a huge endeavor, such as writing a book, by breaking the project down into small, manageable chunks. Yet I'd never applied this helpful, proven approach to the rest of my life. Using Natalie's suggestions and my own process I'd created for my books, I made what I called a living calendar for the huge endeavor known as Life.

It was similar to what I created each time I wrote a book. But instead of having small, daily writing goals that would build up to create a complete book, there were small, daily self-care goals that would build up to form a fully nurtured existence.

Highlighting a period of twenty-one days, I wrote down two doable and specific daily self-care intentions: 1) drink sixty ounces of water, and 2) take a thirty-minute walk outside.

To help with follow-through, I purchased a water jug inscribed with ounce markings and motivational phrases, and I blocked out space in my daily schedule to walk. I vowed to fill my jug and take my walk before opening my computer each morning because being pulled into work first thing was a self-sabotaging pattern for me.

Knowing that my beloved writing calendar had enabled me to write two entire books, I wondered what would result over time through the efforts of my living calendar. As much as I wanted to believe in a promising result, I feared I would not be able to stay consistent given some major life stressors coming up.

Assurance came through an unexpected request from my daughter Avery.

"Can I see my baby book?" she asked one day as we drove home from the store.

Sadly, there was no baby book. Between postpartum depression and an out-of-state move, there was no time or energy for that.

What I did manage to do was fill in a "baby's first-year calendar."

When we got home, I dug it out of the photo album cabinet to show her.

In each calendar box, written in my tired, barely legible handwriting, was a tiny detail about Avery. Reading the brief note about her eating, sleeping, or behavioral habits or an excursion we took that week triggered additional memories for me. I delightedly shared them as Avery soaked up every morsel of information about her baby self.

When we were finished going through it, she looked up at me. "Thank you for taking good care of me," she said.

With tears in my eyes, I glanced at my living calendar—the one I'd made to start taking better care of myself—and felt a renewed sense of hope, which I am honored to share with you now.

Dear Soul Shift Companion, even in the most difficult periods, when facing great obstacles, it is still possible to do something good for our bodies, minds, and souls. One little effort each day can build the foundation for a well-cared-for state of being, which has the potential to ripple far beyond oneself.

Hand in hand, let's keep going . . .

STEPPING-STONE ONE
(A PLACE TO JUST BE)

Dear Soul Shift Companion, I am sure you have begun thinking about where your well-being falls on your daily priority list. If you've realized it's too low or perhaps not making the list at all, do not fear. Instead, let's harness the power of awareness. Not only is awareness the springboard for new, healing habits, but it also comes in unlimited supply.

Over the years, I've found myself constantly having to learn and re-learn how to prioritize my well-being. Yet, with every lapse, my awareness has grown. These days, three key pieces of awareness help me avoid the pitfall of extreme depletion.

After I share these three key pieces of awareness, you will have an opportunity to identify your unique needs, which in turn will prepare you to cultivate a restorative daily practice that works for you.

The first piece of awareness that helps me avoid burnout is having a clear idea of what self-care means to me. There is no one-size-fits-all solution when it comes to looking after yourself, so the more specific you can get about what it means to you, the more intentional you can be about following through.

My personal definition of self-care is this: I turn away from what depletes me, so I can be nourished by what fulfills me.

The list of things that deplete me includes deadlines over which I have no control, excessive social media consumption, being exposed to people who do not respect my boundaries, work assignments that I am not passionate about, skipping meals or eating on the run to get more work completed, responding to text messages, and attending social gatherings where I have to engage in superficial small talk.

Among the things that fulfill me are outdoor walks with no goal, stretching sessions with good music, swinging on swings, practicing loving self-talk, reading historical fiction and contemporary poetry, giving myself as much time as I need, being with animals, and having deep conversations with someone who accepts me unconditionally.

By crafting my personal definition of self-care, I was able to identify specific triggers that cause me to respond in unhealthy, self-sabotaging ways. Insight into my triggers added a second piece of awareness to the puzzle I was sorting out.

For the life of me, I could not understand why I continually fell into a damaging and unhealthy pattern every single time I wrote and published a book. By identifying what depleted me, I realized that some of the expectations and demands in my occupation as an author worked in direct opposition to my meaningful measures of success and worthiness. This tension caused me to act in self-sabotaging ways, such as depriving myself of sleep, getting caught in the comparison trap, consuming excessive caffeine, basing my worth on performance, critiquing my physical appearance, and ignoring warning signs of exhaustion. If ignored long enough, the warning signs became blaring, loud sirens in the form of emotional explosions (like breaking dishes and ignoring health issues).

Discovering my harmful default responses to these triggers helped me gain a third piece of awareness: I needed to set up a support system to turn to during stressful times so I didn't turn on myself. I identified a few trusted people who were willing to offer support and accountability when I was navigating challenging terrain.

These three pieces of awareness—creating my self-care definition, identifying my triggers, and pinpointing my support system—were gained through a series of crises resulting from lapses in self-care.

Yes, you heard that right. I became prepared to properly look after myself only after getting to a very bad place—and having the courage to investigate why. This pattern confirms, once again, why missteps along the Soul Shift journey are not something to be ashamed of or to avoid. Instead, channeling our mistakes into catalysts for growth should be celebrated.

Using the sentence starters below, set yourself up to thrive by identifying key pieces of awareness you may already possess. You may draw pictures or write your responses inside or around the accompanying images.

My definition of self-care is . . .

Some triggers that cause me to respond in unhealthy ways are . . .

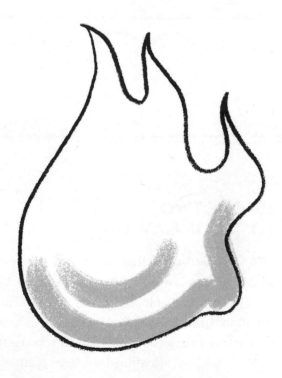

A few things that nourish/replenish/fulfill me are . . .

A potential support system I can identify today is . . .

STEPPING-STONE TWO
(A PLACE TO BECOME AWARE)

Dear Soul Shift Companion, using the preparative measures you have outlined so far, you are now ready to locate the most appropriate starting point for your practice of looking after yourself. Keep in mind there's no judgment in this introspective process. This is a supportive space where you are free to explore pathways on your healing journey that you may not have noticed or realized were accessible.

As you engage with the following check-in questions, you may encounter painful, uncomfortable, or limiting thoughts surrounding the idea of self-care. There's a good chance these are not messages from your authentic self but rather opinions of people or societal messages you have internalized. Should any limiting beliefs surface, simply acknowledge them, perhaps by saying:

> I hear that message, but I don't believe it is coming from me because it doesn't seem to have my best interest in mind. I am going to push that away and listen to the guidance of my soul. It's already brought me so far in this journey; I've begun to see evidence that the guidance of my soul does not steer me wrong. I will be kind and compassionate to myself as I engage with these prompts; I trust that the information I need to proceed is right here, hand over heart.

1. On a scale from 1 to 10 (1 being never and 10 being often), how often do you put other people's needs before your own? How do you think this prioritization impacts your health and well-being?

2. What do you think is your biggest obstacle for meeting your needs on a regular basis? What would it take to remove that obstacle?

3. This reflection involves envisioning what it might actually look like, feel like, or sound like if you were to make yourself a priority today. Some ideas include:
   - Listening to the physical cues your body is sending you to indicate a need—cues like hunger, exhaustion, or thirst—and responding to them instead of putting them off
   - Lowering the bar to seventy or eighty percent on a task you set out to do at one hundred percent
   - Declining a pending request that you've avoided—maybe today is the day you just say, "No, I can't do that."

- Moving your body in a way that feels good to you
- Asking for help with something that feels difficult or overwhelming—perhaps deciding, "I'm going to let somebody in on this; I don't want to carry this alone anymore."

What would it look like, feel like, or sound like if you chose to make yourself a priority today? Be as specific as possible.

If you were to do this right now, what impact might this have on the rest of your day?

STEPPING-STONE THREE
(A PLACE TO PREPARE THE WAY)

Dear Soul Shift Companion, I hope the introspective exercise you just completed has given you some ideas on where to start your Practice in Looking After Yourself. As exciting as it is to locate a starting point to improved well-being, we both know that mastering this practice can be quite challenging. One of the biggest obstacles to self-care is caused by the external pushback we receive when we prioritize ourselves.

Thus, equipping ourselves for this vital practice means accepting the fact that something has to give, and we are probably going to disappoint someone in the process.

"Disappointing people"—despite working on developing a healthy sense of worthiness for many years now, those two words always cause a sense of dread. As you may have gathered from my previous stories, I lived many years believing that disappointing people was *the worst.* But slowly and painfully, I've come to realize that actually *the worst* was living in a state of constantly disappointing myself.

Let me explain . . .

Overextending myself to "keep the peace" disconnected me from my own needs and most everything I hold dear, or My Things That Matter Most. I don't need to list them because they are mine, and you have yours, but one thing remains the same for all of us . . . the things that matter to us must receive nourishment to thrive. Otherwise, they perish, and take us down with them.

I learned it the hard way—and it almost cost me my life. I am trying very hard not to make that mistake again, but let me confess: it's not easy for a recovering people-pleaser to make choices that align with her own values, needs, and limits. When I do, I often disappoint someone. Some go right out and tell me. Others just let me know through their passive-aggressive behavior. In those moments, the old me panics, tells me to fix it, smooth it over, just oblige this one time so I don't have to have a confrontation. That's when I pause and consider what will happen if I fall back into the familiar pattern and just go along with it.

I now know that "going along with it" means denying my own values, needs, and limits. Knowing that that which is not nurtured suffers, I choose myself.

My sister's partner, Chris, gave me some good advice about what to say to myself in these situations: "I'm okay with your disappointment in me."

The first time I used that empowering phrase, I didn't fully believe it myself. I was just slightly okay with that person's disappointment. But once I got through the situation with my self-respect intact, the inner peace I felt put me one hundred percent on board. I eventually adopted the phrase as one of my favorite self-reclamation statements. It took me years to learn the truth; now that I have, I won't forget it: *there's no peace worth keeping if it requires me to betray myself and what I hold most dear.*

Soul Shift Companion, defining and voicing your needs and limits is an important act of self-reclamation—and it's not something anyone else can do for you. You must give it to yourself, one self-honoring choice at a time.

Please take a moment to equip yourself for the practice ahead by:

1. Identifying a task or activity in your current life you could consider relinquishing to create time, energy, and focus to better care for yourself

2. Using the framework below, write down a reclamation phrase you plan to use when your self-prioritization receives pushback (this can be something you plan to say to yourself or to someone else):

I would have time to invest in myself if I were to relinquish
_____ . (For example, "my evening scroll on social media" or "taking work calls at night.")

If this decision disappoints someone, my self-reclamation statement is: _____ .

(An example could be: "This evening habit I've developed is sabotaging my ability to wind down at the end of the day. I have decided I will no longer allow this to happen. I am setting a scroll-free/call-free boundary from 7pm until 7am. I am worthy of protecting my evening peace.")

STEPPING-STONE FOUR
(A PLACE TO STEP OUT)

Dear Soul Shift Companion, it is now time to embark on a Practice in Looking After Yourself. The habit shift that provides the bridge from depleting ourselves to replenishing ourselves is INVESTING in ourselves. As you may have gleaned from my story, what I've found to be most helpful in maintaining the vital practice of looking after myself is to make small, attainable goals and put them in writing.

The living calendar you are about to create does just that.

As with the other practices we have covered in our journey, it's the small-step shifts that create the positive and lasting transformation we seek. A Practice in Looking After Yourself is not reserved for times when it's convenient; this practice is most beneficial when it's performed daily. Through daily practice, caring for yourself will start to feel as natural and routine as it does to care for others.

Let's begin crafting our living calendar by identifying a few small self-care investments you could make today. To help form ideas, I'm going to offer a few suggestions from an article I refer to on a monthly basis. Entitled "50 Ways Happier and Healthier People Live On Their Own Terms," the article is by organizational psychologist and motivational author Dr. Benjamin Hardy.

- Wait at least sixty to ninety minutes before checking your email and social media after you wake up
- Have no more than three items on your to-do list today
- Make your bed
- Write and place a short, thoughtful note for someone
- Write in your journal for five minutes
- Get seven or more hours of sleep tonight

Did any of those intentions resonate with you or spark your own self-care ideas? If so, make a note next to them.

Now I'd like you to draw a rectangle with twenty-one boxes inside the front flap of the book, or if you prefer you can print out a blank calendar template from the Internet to tape inside the book. (Make sure the boxes are large enough to write a few words inside.)

Next, decide on two self-care goals to pursue for the next twenty-one days. I use twenty-one days because I find a three-week commitment to be both manageable and achievable. Although the "twenty-one days to form a habit" idea has been proven a myth, it IS a fact that habits are learned through repetition. Twenty-one days of repeating a self-care act has proven to be quite effective for me, but please know you can shorten or lengthen the time frame as you see fit.

Once you decide your goal(s), jot them down inside the blank calendar boxes. Plan to take thirty seconds each day to assess your goals. I draw a smiley face when I complete a goal and write nothing when I don't. The reason I do not draw a sad face for days I do not meet a goal is because shame and condemnation are not motivating. What is motivating? Grace, compassion, belief, and understanding. If you aren't able to fulfill an intention, try to determine what got in the way and what you might do differently the next day to ensure you make the investment of looking after yourself.

Keep in mind, these small actions may not give instant results, especially when years of stress and unhealthy habits have built up, but don't underestimate the impact of these investments over time. Be mindful of the small, incremental improvements you notice, like being irritable a little less often, feeling a little less tired, feeling more limber or more flexible. It may not be evident right away, but these small shifts can have immeasurable impacts on your life and those around you.

After the twenty-one-day period has passed, review your living calendar. Ask yourself questions: *What worked? What didn't? What would you like to change? What would you like to continue? Is it time to add another loving self-care practice to your daily routine?*

Whether you continue to add new goals or maintain the ones you already have in place, these habitual actions will serve as a supportive foundation when you encounter triggering territories and challenging times.

For me, this healing practice revealed its value during the writing of my fourth book. Throughout the daunting process, I continually invested in myself—which enabled me to support my daughter, Avery, as she experienced a devastating setback in her ongoing treatment for severe scoliosis.

On my living calendar, I'd committed to keeping up my daily walking routine. I defined it as, "Walk whenever and wherever you can, even if it's just for a few minutes."

Because of those specifics, one day I chose to explore the outdoors during Avery's guitar lesson rather than run errands or work in my car.

While exploring the unfamiliar area, I discovered a path that led to a bench swing placed on the bank of the Chattahoochee River. I honestly thought I was dreaming—of all the things I could encounter in that challenging season in my life, I was guided to the very thing that gave me peace and comfort as a child.

I sat down and swayed forward and backward, marveling, breathing, listening, praying, crying, and connecting to my heart. When I got up twenty minutes later, my burdens were lighter and my path was clearer.

I ended up visiting that bench swing once a week as I completed the manuscript for my fourth book and accompanied Avery through extensive hospital visits and therapies. That weekly commitment to invest in my well-being enabled me to see injustices I had neglected to see before, specifically the wide disparities in the health status of different social and ethnic groups.

As Avery and I ventured into large metropolitan areas for appointments each week, we saw how people in marginalized communities with the same needs as my family did not have access to the same resources or receive the same treatment. This spurred my daughter and me to begin attending social justice gatherings so we could learn how to use our unearned privilege to raise awareness and dismantle the inequity built into health systems.

After decades of neglecting myself to the point where I could be of service to no one, being able to participate in effective activism while supporting my daughter felt like hope. Being able to foster connection with Avery, as well as the greater community, offered us a way to see beyond our own pain. It is with great joy that I share this awakening with you, one that started as a commitment in one tiny calendar box.

Dear Soul Shift Companion, in a world that looks for the quick fix . . . celebrates powering through pain . . . resists rest and glorifies busyness, we often lose sight of the bigger picture. Through intentional self-care practices, we can be better equipped to advocate for ourselves and others.

Today, I extend my hand and offer you compassion and support for the steps ahead. I hope you'll accept because filling your cup fills mine, too. Let's do it together.

Please set an intention right now to look after yourself by writing down a phrase, takeaway, or tool from this practice area that you plan to use right away:

After implementing it in your daily life, be sure to draw a colorful line or symbol on your living map. Even small investments in well-being widen the path to healing and hope.

Please grab a sticky note and write down the healing truth that we uncovered today. Post this visual reminder where you can see it often.

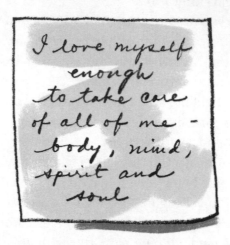

A PEACEFUL SPOT

(a Place to Let Things Sink In)

Stories:

INVEST IN PIECES OF WORTHINESS

INVEST IN CALMING EXERCISES

INVEST IN SIDES OF SAFETY

Invest in Pieces of Worthiness

After going years without making the world's best key lime pie, I made it twice in one month's time.

I became aware this pie existed after having kidney surgery in July of 2015. A neighbor I didn't know very well at the time unexpectedly dropped it off at my house.

I had absolutely no appetite, but this cool, creamy pie actually sounded quite good. I ate my share and then some, much to my family's disappointment.

Long after the pie was gone, the lingering impact of the gesture remained. I was struck by the fact that my neighbor deemed me worthy of the time, effort, and ingredients required to bake that beautiful pie.

Some loving gestures catch us at the right time, filling an emotional emptiness we didn't know we had. The pie was more than just pie; it carried meaning.

I found myself digging out my neighbor's recipe on Easter Sunday and then again, a few weeks later, for my mother-in-law's visit.

"You've been making this pie a lot," my family happily noticed.

I noticed, too—and I wondered if there was an underlying reason.

An exchange with a friend at the cluster mailboxes in our neighborhood clued me in. When she saw me limping, she asked how things were going with my foot.

I unexpectedly blurted out that none of the therapies had worked, so I was going to need surgery.

"Promise me you'll tell me the procedure date when it gets scheduled," my friend implored.

Promise me. Those were her exact words.

She knew . . .

I am inclined to suffer in silence rather than have anyone go to any trouble for me.

I am inclined to suggest support be extended to those who have greater needs than I do.

I am inclined to be the one who helps, not the one who *is* helped.

That's when my friend placed her hand over her heart and said, "It would be my honor to show up for you."

My eyes started watering.

Honor.

I know about that—to BE the pie bearer is an honor.

A few years ago my cat, Banjo, was very sick. This came up in a tearful conversation with the cashier in the supermarket checkout line and, to my surprise, she walked around the counter to hug me and offer support. When I later heard this woman, Ms. Suna, had been hospitalized, I visited her while she recuperated. I was honored to reciprocate her kindness to me. I ended up writing a letter to the CEO of the grocery store chain to ensure he knew about this remarkable woman who cares for all of her customers like she cared for me that day.

From that moment on, Ms. Suna called me her "angel."

When she had to stop working at the store a few months ago due to health issues, she gave me her address and phone number and told me to visit anytime.

Now when I drive to her home with flowers and cards, I think about the photo she showed me of herself in her younger days.

"I used to be beautiful," she said wistfully.

It is my honor to make sure she knows she is STILL beautiful and worthy of flowers and citrus streusel bread and friendship and prayers.

Ms. Suna says my visits seem to come just when she needs to know she has not been forgotten.

I think about the pie that wasn't only a pie, but also a delicious reminder that being a willing and gracious receiver is a gift in itself.

In Jessica Lahey's remarkable book *The Addiction Inoculation*, there's a section I don't think I'll ever forget. In it, Jessica offers advice to teens who suspect a peer may have substance abuse issues. "Be the first piece of the puzzle," she writes. "Hardly anyone stops drinking or using drugs when the first person mentions there might be a problem, and it may not be until the fiftieth person says something. But without person one through forty-nine, there is no fiftieth person."

I can't seem to stop thinking about that metaphor. I wonder if it works with other things, like:

Worthiness

Significance

Hope

Healing

I think about the pie bearers—at some point one of them offers the piece that makes the belief finally sink in . . .

I am worth the trouble.

I am worth the time.

I am worthy of the best ingredients.

I am worthy of recognition from the CEO.

I am worthy of an activity that boosts my endorphins.

I am worthy of having my needs met.

I am worthy of a pain-free life.

The day that belief finally sinks in might just be the day . . .

the long-overdue appointment is made

the brave first step is taken

the help is accepted

the boundary is set

the bike ride is taken

the glass is filled

the answer becomes clear

All of this because someone filled an emotional emptiness with a belief the hurting person didn't even know was missing.

For as long as I am fortunate to live, I will never underestimate the power of being the pie bearer; nor will I ever underestimate the power in receiving the pie. No matter what side you're on, you are worthy of a big, beautiful slice.

Notes to Ponder

I deemed myself worthy by investing a "piece"
of _____ when I . . .

I validated the worth of someone else by offering
a "piece" of _____ when I . . .

Invest in Calming Exercises

While I was working out of town for a week one summer, Natalie oversaw putting our rambunctious four-year-old cat, Paisley, to bed each night.

Born outside an apartment complex whose manager was intent on destroying him and his siblings until we rescued him, Paisley always had to be on high alert . . . which may explain why our hyperactive kitty doesn't rest easily.

Anticipating that Paisley's anxiety would be off the charts while I was gone, my daughter decided to brush him to sleep.

Now, I wouldn't have believed the relaxed state of this cat had Natalie not sent a video of him sprawled out on his back, limp as a noodle, nearly drooling on himself.

It was quite entertaining to watch these nightly videos. And once I was back home, I got to see it in person.

Paisley jumped up next to me while I was watching TV and assumed the brushing position. Being a good cat mom, I obliged.

As I gently brushed his furry belly, tiny armpits, and other places most cats deem off limits, I marveled.

How can a little brush have this effect? I wondered.

And then I remembered . . . in the toughest school year of my special education career, the co-teacher and I were trained by the occupational therapist on how to use the Wilbarger Brushing Protocol, a therapy proven to be beneficial for children with immature nervous systems.

When the occupational therapist handed us three-inch surgical brushes that resembled vegetable scrubbers and voiced a vote of confidence, my colleague and I looked at each other skeptically. But when you're desperate, you'll grasp for any thread of hope. The first three weeks of school hadn't just been challenging for us as educators; they'd been soul-crushing. The proposed curriculum for this group of students quickly felt like a cruel joke. Teaching mathematics and language arts lessons was simply out of the question when we were dodging flying chairs and breaking up fist fights. The co-teacher and I quickly understood why these twelve particular students had exhausted all other special education resources in the district: our classroom was their last chance to stay at school.

The next day, I explained to the students that a brushing regimen would be performed on their arms, legs, and back for ten minutes each day.

At first, the sensation of the brush upon their skin caused the children to erupt in fits of laughter. But with every motion of the brush, the room grew quieter. For the first time in weeks, there was peace. My co-teacher and I exchanged looks of disbelief. With tears of hope in my eyes, I wondered, *Could this really work?*

Yes.

Within days, we saw improvement in all of our students, but the exercise seemed to have the most impact on our students with explosive temperaments. Within minutes of initiating the brushing protocol, defensiveness left the room and trust showed up.

After a ten-minute brushing session, our students were able to focus on brief academic lessons and complete their work. It was miraculous. In our classroom these little brushes became more valuable than gold; we ordered them in bulk.

I'll never forget the morning our most challenging student came bursting into the classroom. He spouted off something about getting in trouble on the bus and how he wanted to punch the bus driver in the face . . . but he didn't. Without taking a breath, he angrily declared, "I need brushing!"

From that point on, brushing became our students' go-to for stress. When tension began mounting, we'd offer a brushing session. Rather than ripping apart the classroom or attacking another student, students began to choose to go to the "relaxation rug" to be brushed.

On that rug was where the real miracle happened.

While gathered in a circle, waiting their turn to be brushed, the children began sharing their lived experiences. As pain and worry poured out into our palms, it was difficult to remain stoic. But this wasn't about me or my feelings—it was about making the students feel seen . . . heard . . . safe. There on that rug, the walls they'd built to protect themselves seemed to come down so healing could enter.

Holding the cat brush in my hand reminded me of this miracle . . . and what a good time to remember the power of connection when it comes to processing trauma—in both animals and humans.

The global crisis resulting from the COVID-19 pandemic has caused uncertainty, loneliness, pain, stress, and despair to build up in incomprehensible ways. Perhaps you are experiencing for yourself how difficult it is to learn, perform, sleep, and engage when you've had your guard up for so long.

That's why engaging in some calming exercise needs to be a priority each day—perhaps now more than ever before. Whether it's visualizing yourself in your happy place, coloring with crayons, or speaking loving affirmations, you give yourself a real shot at bringing comfort and healing to the walled-up places within.

Notes to Ponder

Like brushing did for the students, I am able to bring a sense of physical comfort to myself when I . . .

I invested in a calming exercise when I . . .

Invest in Sides of Safety

When Avery reported that she'd successfully slept in her uncomfortable scoliosis brace until 4:30 a.m., the longest she'd slept in it since she began the nightly routine, I had one question.

"What do you think made the difference?"

Avery did not hesitate.

"Being in the water."

Around sunset the night before, we'd gone to the neighborhood pool to swim, stretch, float, and talk.

Because Avery felt certain that the water made the difference, we started visiting the neighborhood pool regularly. And I began to notice that Avery always did the same thing before starting her swimming routine. When she first got in the pool, she swam to the corners of the pool and rescued the bugs floating on top of the water. Many were no longer alive, but she scooped them up anyway, set them gently on the cement, and watched intently for a sign of life.

One morning, after rescuing three bugs, Avery swam into the deepest waters, where she could not touch the bottom. While I watched, she transported a bug in her open hand while propelling herself forward with her free hand and strong legs, her head barely above the water. As the bug rested in Avery's loving hand—on its way to the side of safety—so, too, Avery was being held in loving hands. Like the bugs being scooped up in love, she, too, no longer had to struggle, but was being brought to a place of refuge and healing in her own right.

Sensing me watching, she called out, "It's a little heart, but it's a heart . . . and we should do everything we can to keep it beating."

Yes, my own heart emphatically agreed.

I marveled at the way empathy seems to grow when human beings experience personal pain and how that empathy spurs action to ease another's pain.

"We should do everything we can to keep it beating . . ."

Even if it means experiencing inconvenience.

Even it is means exposing ourselves to judgment or rejection.

Even if it means navigating terrain that we have previously avoided out of fear.

Even if the outcome is not what we had hoped for.

Because, as we reach for that one beating heart, we also reach for our own. While we watch expectantly for signs of well-being, we temporarily feel better.

It is in the journey from the deep end to the side of safety, one hand propelling us forward and the other holding hope for someone else, that we gain momentum, information, and experience. That hope we are creating for another soul suddenly becomes ours, too.

During one of our swimming sessions, Avery voiced a conclusion she had reached: "Having scoliosis is nothing to be ashamed of. Maybe someday I'll talk about how hard it was and what helped me through it. I will definitely be singing about it, although putting it into words that are relatable may be hard," she speculated.

And just as I was about to offer some advice, Avery said, "But I know I'll find a way."

Yes, my child; I have no doubt you will.

202

As I've said before, we all have songs. And each day, new lines and lyrics are being written; new chapters and choruses are beginning and ending. And today, this is my anthem, carried back from the deep end to the wall of refuge. May it revive your weary heart.

Anthem from the Deep End

It is good to envision a positive outcome at the end of this trial, but don't forget to take it one calendar box at a time.

It is good to keep propelling yourself forward, but don't forget to stop to float . . . marvel . . . notice . . . and breathe.

It is good to be open to the messages of your heart, mind, and dreams, but don't forget fear diminishes in swaying swings, soft fur, and brave admissions.

It is good to reach for one beating heart, but when a loving hand comes swooping into the deep end, stop treading water and rest in the hands of love.

Such respite is not too good to be true; it is just how much you are loved.

Notes to Ponder

The "deep end" for me is . . .

The "side of safety" for me is . . .

I stopped propelling myself forward and
invested in "float time" when I . . .

ASSURANCE FOR YOUR POCKET

Today offers you the chance to create new, healthy rhythms in a culture that conditions us to deny self-care to the point of great harm. "But I am discouraged," I hear you say, "so why should I keep trying?" In response, I lovingly offer you these reminders.

- Because someone breathes easier when you show up (do not underestimate the significance of this)
- Because your actual efforts, no matter how small or imperfect, hold far more power to create change than mere words
- Because your presence is enough (that's right: throw the "standards" out the window—you showing up, day after day, *is* enough)
- Because things *are* going to get better, and won't it be glorious to be there when they do?
- Because you have come too far to stop now

Dear Soul Shift Companion, when in doubt, hydrate your weary heart with this cool canteen of loving truths:

Rest if you need to—those who try are worthy of pause.

Cry if you need to—those who try do not need to be strong all the time.

Vent if you need to—those who try have a right to release their frustration; they carry enough as it is.

Celebrate if you need to—those who try deserve recognition cupcakes, flowers, and notes.

Accept yourself if you need to—those who try are entitled to loving themselves right where they are.

And where you are right now, brave self, is quite remarkable.

I see you trying, and I salute you.

PRACTICE EIGHT
OFFERING YOUR GIFT TO THE WORLD

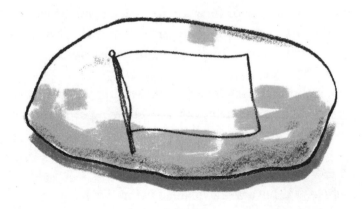

START HERE...

When courage steps forward, we see vulnerability is not a weakness. In the light of a shared struggle, there is strength.

When courage steps forward, we see the unexpected ways we've been prepared for this moment. As our senses fill with awe, there is less room for fear.

When courage steps forward, small details become lifelines for coping with unknowns. Their certainties ground us in peace, even when our voice shakes.

When courage steps forward, people come together to do things they could not do alone. Hope is doubled; opportunity is multiplied.

When courage steps forward, miracles result as we participate in something bigger than ourselves. A spark is ignited when our gift fills a need in the world.

When courage steps forward, our willingness to be brave becomes the ultimate advantage, allowing us to reclaim the joy within ourselves.

Courage, please step forward.
Refuse to believe we have failed before we have even begun.
New beginnings are not found in fear.
They emerge from a place of love.

Courage, please step forward.
Show us how our brave efforts can forge groundbreaking paths, wide enough for humankind to walk side by side.

MILESTONE ALERT!

I f you read this guide in chronological order, you have now reached the final area of exploration in our Soul Shift journey. Some might view the Practice of Offering Your Gift to the World as the focal point in the garden. Whether it's a stunning fountain, a gazebo adorned with white lights, or a cheery red bench, a garden's focal point captures the eye, making sure all the attention is on the standout area and away from the less appealing aspects of the landscape.

The heart of the Soul Shift journey, like the focal point of a garden, draws us in. Witnessing human beings showcase their purpose in the world *is* quite captivating, but it can also be downright intimidating. Focusing only on people's gifts in their glorious splendor means we do not see the whole landscape; namely, how did those gifts develop? We know the heart of the garden wasn't cultivated without some effort; likewise, until we understand the obstacles others faced and overcame, it can be difficult to relate to their accomplishments or believe we are equally capable of developing such a flourishing area in our own life.

Simply reading the title of this practice area may have caused you to want to retreat. Perhaps you read the words "your gift to the world" and felt instantly uncomfortable. Perhaps you had questions, valid concerns like: *But what if I don't know what my gift is? What if I'm scared to try? What if I have no support? What if I feel like I've already missed my chance?*

Let me assure you, we will get to the bottom of these important questions because this practice is about so much more than cultivating the heart of the journey; it's the essence of reclaiming your joy. Why? Because **our gifts reflect who we are at our innermost core.** When we hide, deny, or forgo using our gifts, it is natural to feel despondent and unfulfilled, as if something is missing. On the other hand, using our gifts cultivates peace, purpose, and happiness in our lives, and even provides opportunities for others to contribute their gifts. This ripple effect builds a more humane, inclusive, and equitable world.

Although our final area of exploration holds the focal point of the garden, we must first expand our view to include the far-too-often unacknowledged effort required to see it flourish. By giving you a bird's-eye view, I hope you will see that even the human writing these words still asks herself the same questions you are likely pondering for yourself. *Am I capable? Do I have anything to contribute?* Yes, doubt and fear still reappear for me when offering my gift to the world, but I refuse to let them stop me from showing up. May the details I expose in the area ahead help you begin to envision the heart of your living garden, one that is thriving in the light of self-reclamation.

Let's get started . . .

After my casserole dish outburst that led to the discovery of a giant kidney stone and an arduous medical journey, two truths became clear:

1. The world will not give me permission to stop and breathe. I am the only one who can give this to myself.

2. If I am going to have a real shot at connecting to places and people that bring me peace, joy, and restoration, I have to make space and time to do so. No one is going to make these investments for me.

With all of my hard-earned awareness at hand, I designated one afternoon a week to engage in an enjoyable activity that was not work related and got me out of the house, so I'd be less tempted by unfinished tasks. I chose Sunday because my daughters were available to join me, and the timing could provide a nice transition into a new week. The theme of Sunday afternoons became this: Go where your heart leads. No schedule. No hurry. No expectations. Just listen to your heart's desires.

Soon, that directive led me to a local cat shelter in my area called "All About Cats." It had become a Sunday tradition for my daughters and me to visit cats there.

During one visit, the owner of the shelter, Kristy, happened to be there. We were excited to see her because we had a lot of questions. Our conversation went something like this:

"Hello . . . we were just wondering . . . where's Snowball? Did she get adopted this week? We noticed Odie's been here awhile—what's his story? Harper's looking a little depressed. Is she okay?"

For an uncomfortably long moment, Kristy just stared at us. I wondered if she was going to call security and report a cat stalker in aisle seven.

But instead, she smiled and said, "Would you and your daughters like to volunteer here? We really could use some nice people who care about cats."

As elated as I was by this opportunity, I felt immediately conflicted. *But wait . . . my brain said . . . this wasn't the plan! You are supposed to be creating breathing room on Sundays, not filling them with obligations!*

I couldn't deny the painful truth I was now keenly aware of: **offering my gift to this cause will only deplete me.**

I politely thanked Kristy and let her know we'd think about her invitation.

I followed through with my promise, thinking about the opportunity more than I expected I would. In fact, the more I thought about this chance encounter and the rare invitation to care for homeless animals in the company of my daughters, the more intrigued I became. For some reason, this opportunity felt vastly different than the other requests I was bombarded with day after day. It felt more like an opportunity than an obligation, and that nudge on my heart convinced me to say yes.

It didn't take long for my decision to be confirmed. Right away, I noticed something fascinating. My two daughters, who have extremely different personalities and approaches to life, quickly found their niche. Natalie joyfully cleaned, scrubbed, organized, and enhanced while Avery conversed, cuddled, played, and sang. But here's the thing: neither way was wrong. Both approaches were impactful. Each child had a purpose and a unique contribution to make at the shelter.

But Natalie and Avery were not the only ones who found a place there. I found I couldn't bear the way visitors' faces fell when they read the sign, "Cleaning in progress, please come back later." So, I would crack the door and ask if they'd like to come in. Not everyone accepted, but when they did, I'd find myself listening to someone's vulnerable story, one that clearly needed to be heard. I found it incredibly comforting to simply connect as one human being to another. Being strangers, we had no past baggage or future expectation to sabotage our present, shared moment.

When there were no visitors, I simply comforted the cats. I cherished these moments, often remembering my younger self who could never walk by a stray cat without talking to it. Back then, I was told not to touch unfamiliar animals because they might be sick or aggressive, so being able to hold and love these vulnerable creatures now filled me with peace.

A few weeks in, Natalie downloaded photos from our visits. I was pleased, though not surprised, by the expression of peace, serenity, fulfillment, joy, and contentment resting on my face in the pictures. It reminded me so much of my eight-year-old self . . . the mixtape maker, animal lover, notebook filler with dreams of becoming an author. In the cat shelter photos, I could clearly see my Dreamer Girl shining through my grown-up self.

I'd assumed that volunteering at the cat shelter would deplete me as so many service opportunities had before, but that was not the case. Each time we were due for a visit, it didn't matter how much I had going on in my life, I felt grateful and excited to go. I knew I would come away feeling fulfilled after connecting with animals, engaging with my daughters, and hearing uplifting stories of resilience and recovery from potential adopters.

Tears filled my eyes as a new, healing, two-part truth surfaced:

When you go where your heart calls you to go, you experience true fulfillment. You go to be a gift to the world, yet you are the one who is given a gift.

When you go
where your heart
calls you
to go, you
experience true
fulfillment

The cat shelter quickly became a place of peace for me, which was why I didn't tell anyone there about my work as an author or speaker. I simply wanted to be known there as Rachel, Cat Whisperer, Soul-Builder, Loving Listener.

For five solid years I maintained professional anonymity at the cat shelter. Then, one day, word got out that I'd published several books and was a public speaker.

Two lovely volunteers in charge of fundraising for the shelter approached me.

"Rachel, we've read your work, and it's so beautiful. Would you be willing to speak at our fundraising event? It would contribute immensely to the shelter," Pam and Michelle said.

When I tell you that panic gripped me, that is not an understatement. I began sweating profusely and trying to think of a way out.

I was honestly a bit surprised by these feelings. By that time in my career, I'd spoken at countless events across the country. But in the back of mind, I knew this would be my first speaking event in the city where I'd resided for seven years. The thought of sharing painful details of my past with my next-door neighbors felt a bit like running naked down the street. I cannot adequately express how much I did not want to speak at this event. But then I thought about the cats. They desperately needed the funding, and I had a gift I could offer that could help them.

Recognizing that my acceptance of this request would classify as a *scary yes*, I knew I needed a support system in place. I asked my daughters to participate in the event with me. Natalie, with her superior organization and entrepreneurial skills, agreed to run the book table. Avery, with her welcoming personality and musical talent, agreed to weave songs into my talk.

At this point, I could cut right to the chase and tell you the cat shelter fundraiser was beautifully received and hugely successful. Those things would all be true, but I promised to show you more than the appealing focal point of the journey. Because when we see people bravely, even radiantly, sharing their gifts, we need to remember that what we do not see is equally important. That's where I am taking you now, into the less attractive areas of a flourishing garden. It is my hope that my transparency helps you grow more confident as you progress on your own journey and allow yourself to be open to possibilities you never imagined for your life.

Let's keep going . . .

A BIRD'S-EYE VIEW

A few weeks before the fundraiser, I started having terrible nightmares, which is how my anxiety often manifests. I decided to confide in Natalie, who was fifteen years old at the time.

"I am really scared to do this speaking event because all these people we know are going to be there, and I'm afraid they will judge me."

"I know how that feels, Mom," Natalie said. Sensing my emotionally reserved daughter was about to give me a rare glimpse into her inner world, I physically leaned in, hoping she'd see how much she was already helping me. Natalie proceeded to describe how she tends to "get in her head" when she's on the block before a swimming event, which rattles her confidence. So, she began using a grounding technique. By listening to the sound of the water in the pool, she is able to imagine herself in her favorite safe, restorative place: the beach. Her mind stops racing with thoughts, and she is able to connect to her body and trust in its capableness.

"And that is what you will do, Mom," Natalie said. "When you get on stage, you will imagine yourself talking to your friend Kerry, who accepts you unconditionally. By imagining yourself talking to her, your words will flow from your heart."

Natalie also suggested I keep a *brave journal* in the days leading up to the event. After she showed me her notebook filled with inspiring quotes that helped her stretch beyond her comfort zone, I designated a journal for this purpose. Inspired by my exchange with Natalie, the first thing I wrote in my *brave journal* was this:

When courage steps forward, we see vulnerability is not a weakness.

In the light of a shared struggle, there is strength.

On the morning of the event, I felt strangely at peace. This time, it was Avery who was nervous. On the day she was due to perform in front of the largest audience of her life, Avery had woken up with a scratchy throat.

She came to me with a look of panic in her eyes. Worried, she asked, "What if I can't sing like I normally do?"

With absolute certainty, I said, "I think the best thing you can do right now is pack up your guitar, drink some warm tea, and trust your voice and your message. Even if they're a little shaky or out of tune, I believe they are exactly what someone needs to hear today."

Avery hugged me and she repeated the words I'd said to her so many times throughout her medical ordeal: "I'm going to trust that things will be okay. And if they're not, I'm going to trust I'll be able to handle them."

From that conversation, I added a second discovery to my *brave journal*:

When courage steps forward, we see what faith and trust look like in action.

When we surrender control, we're able to grasp what's needed to do our job.

Shortly after we arrived at the venue where the event was going to be held, Avery's friend Laila arrived. After greeting each other with hugs, the duo set off to explore the facility. Knowing how popular Avery's informal singing and strumming videos were becoming on the Internet, Laila confidently said, "Don't worry. I'll protect you from any potential stalkers."

It wasn't long before the pair came running back into the room where I was preparing. They showed me an exquisite leather journal that had just been given to Avery by a lovely teenager who traveled four hours with her sister and mom to attend the event.

Avery read the quote inscribed on the journal out loud:

"If you have good thoughts they will shine out of your face
like sunbeams and you will always look lovely."
—Roald Dahl

Chills radiated throughout my body. While visiting her aunt Rebecca in North Carolina, Avery saw that quote painted on a giant canvas in a restaurant bathroom. After reciting it several times, she asked me to take her picture standing beneath it. Since that moment, the quote held a special place in her heart, and no one knew this but us.

After this exchange, I added a third fear-fighting discovery to my *brave journal*:

When courage steps forward, we often find someone has already anticipated our arrival.

To be known by heart confirms we are in the right place.

When the girls left the room, I could hear the sound of people filling the venue. The crowd was bigger than I had anticipated, and my heart began racing. Just then, Laila's mom, Britt, peeked in to check on me. When she hugged me, my worries came pouring out.

"This is a new talk I have never given. I have to be the most vulnerable I've ever been. My kids are here. My friends are here. I'm scared," I confessed.

Britt looked directly into my face and said, "Rachel, you've been on the *Today Show*! Remember? Millions of people watched you speak your truth so beautifully! If you can do that, then you can do this!"

I have a unique gift for compartmentalizing stressful moments in my memory, so I would have never instinctively recalled that experience to give me strength. I felt my face break into a much-needed smile as I remembered navigating the crowded streets of New York City to sit on the *Today Show* couch, baring my soul to the hosts and millions of viewers. Somehow Britt knew that triumph was just the confidence-building reminder I needed.

From that exchange, I wrote down a fourth discovery in my *brave journal*:

When courage steps forward, we see the unexpected ways we've been prepared for this moment.

As our senses fill with awe, there is less room for fear.

When the hour-long presentation ended, friends came forward to say they couldn't believe it was the first time Avery and I presented together. They commented on how naturally our gifts fit together and how deeply they resonated.

I made a mental note to tell Avery's guitar instructor, Corey, how much his help with song transitions and stage presence benefited our presentation. When Avery's hair had gotten in her eye during one of our practice sessions, Corey suggested she consider tying it back.

He said, "I know it sounds silly to talk about your hair, but there will be so many things outside your control when you perform. So, if there's anything you *can* manage ahead of time, do it to give yourself added peace."

On the morning of the event, Corey's words resonated. With steady hands, Avery pulled back the sides of her hair into a pink scrunchy and then added a few hairpins for extra security.

From this outcome, I wrote a fifth discovery in my *brave journal*:

When courage steps forward, small details become lifelines to cope with the unknowns.

They ground us in peace even when our voice gets shaky.

Halfway through the book signing, a young woman who'd taken my online course approached me. Although she'd told me she was planning to fly in from out of state to attend the event, seeing her actually standing there felt miraculous. I'd met her at a previous speaking event in Ohio and would never forget our encounter. With visibly shaking hands, she explained how my work was helping her reparent her inner child after being rejected by the two people she counted on to love her unconditionally. This young woman's words had fueled me to write a book on how adults can become trustworthy and relatable guides for children and teens as they navigate a tricky world.

Seeing this brave woman at the cat shelter benefit gave me a chance to say something very important to her: "I know sometimes you wonder if your life matters," I said, placing the published book in her hands. "In those moments, I want you to open these pages and remember *you* provided the fuel I needed to start writing this book."

This special interaction led me to write the sixth discovery in my *brave journal*:

> **When courage steps forward, people are brought together to do things they could not do alone.**
>
> **Hope is doubled; opportunity is multiplied.**

At the end of the five-hour function, my daughters and I packed up all of our equipment and headed out to our car. As soon as she closed the door, Avery let out a mammoth-sized exhale.

"Is this how you always feel after a speaking event?" she asked, slipping off her shoes and wiggling her feet.

"Do you mean completely exhausted but in the best possible way?" I asked.

"Yes!" Avery laughed. "When can we do it again?"

From Avery's remark, a seventh discovery was added to my *brave journal*:

> **When courage steps forward, we see miracles form when we do something bigger than ourselves.**
>
> **A fire is ignited within when our inherent gift fills a need in the world.**

Despite the emotional challenges and intense effort required of her, Avery's response to the event illustrated the findings of Dr. William Damon, one of the world's leading scholars of human development.

"Kids who have a strong sense of purpose and find what they're doing to be meaningful can expend enormous amounts of energy, take on huge challenges, and meet all kinds of demands, and are quite joyful about what they're doing," he writes in his book *The Path to Purpose*. "All stress is not created equal, and with a sense of purpose, there are built-in protective factors against depression and a host of anxiety disorders."

Throughout my special education career and classroom interviews as an author, I have seen proof of Dr. Damon's findings. I have also found that his theory applies to adults. Using your passions, talents, and care for the world in ways that infuse your life with meaning is hugely beneficial at any age. Thankfully, it is never too late to begin this purpose-identifying process, which is why the practices you've learned in the Soul Shift journey are so valuable. Deciding you won't live a life that is overscheduled and undervalued . . . viewing trials, mistakes, and missteps as stepping-stones . . . establishing healthy boundaries and self-care habits . . . these are just a few of the path-clearing tools you now possess. With them, you are prepared to discover the heart of your journey where you feel most alive.

Did you hear that? **You are ready**.

That's right: this exploration area does not have a Stepping-Stone One because *you already possess what is needed to offer your gift to the world*. You just need to tap into the courage inside you and simply show up.

You are ready because you aren't doing this alone. Think about the people who showed up for the cat shelter fundraiser and used their unique gifts to bring it to life—from Laila to the journal giver . . . from Laila's mom to the guitar instructor . . . from the book signing attendee to every person in attendance, including the encouraging soul nodding at me from the back of the room. Every single individual who offered their gift that day became part of a beautiful whole that was so much more powerful than any one person could have been on their own.

I can assure you, not one of these individuals consciously prepared to play the role they did that day; they simply stepped forward when their heart indicated they had something to contribute. And because they did, remarkable things happened.

Remarkable things—those two words deserve a pause . . . and an explanation.

The concept of "remarkable things" has been a driving force throughout my entire Soul Shift journey. They were unexpectedly gifted to me during one of my first media interviews about my blog, *Hands Free Mama*, which unexpectedly captivated a large readership in a short amount of time.

At a tiny coffee shop in downtown Birmingham, Alabama, a twenty-something magazine editor asked me how my Hands Free journey started. Hesitantly, I told her about the kiss-on-the-hand moment with Avery. I honestly didn't think the young writer was going to understand the life-changing magnitude of that simple gesture.

Needless to say, I was shocked when she leaned in and offered the most beautiful admission over the tops of our coffee cups.

"I love to make art in my spare time," the editor vulnerably shared, "and I *just* painted my favorite quote by novelist Jon McGregor. Your story makes me think of that quote."

She then closed her eyes and thought for a moment, as if wanting to get the words just right. In a low, soothing voice reserved for sacred spaces, the woman recited, "If nobody speaks of remarkable things, how can they be called remarkable?"

Dear Soul Shift Companion, this entire practice is about life's *remarkable things*. They don't just happen; they are *created* when our heart recognizes a place where we have something to offer . . . and we courageously step forward.

Courage is the only antidote to fear. When we stare fear of failure and rejection in the face and change the narrative, we learn that it has been a matter of perspective all along. Suddenly, we find ourselves saying things like:

"I am scared, but I'm showing up anyway . . . "

"I feel like this invitation is an opportunity, not a burden . . ."

"I'm exhausted in the best possible way! When can I do it again?"

This realization inspired the eighth and most powerful purpose-guiding discovery that now lives in my *brave journal*:

When courage steps forward, we see that our willingness to be brave becomes the ultimate fuel, allowing us to spark the long-lost joy within ourselves.

May this truth come to reside in your *brave journal*, dear traveling companion, and may it come alive in your life.

I see light ahead.

STEPPING-STONE TWO
(A PLACE TO BECOME AWARE)

Dear Soul Shift Companion, the check-in questions below are designed to help you access your internal guidance system so you can begin to take steps in the most meaningful direction for you. Understanding what you value most can help narrow down your life's passion and purpose to something manageable that also resonates with you. Identifying your personal strengths and/or times in your life when you lacked support can help guide you toward something you really care about.

Although negative past experiences and internalized messages of doubt and inadequacy may surface throughout this exercise, I encourage you to gently acknowledge and then release them. Perhaps say to yourself, "That is not the direction I am heading today," and then envision a new, uncharted, curiosity-rich path ahead to leisurely explore. Keep in mind, even one tiny insight found here can change your perspective of the entire horizon.

1. What are you really good at? Or, what do other people say you do that is special or helpful?

2. Think about a hardship you went through in your life . . .
   Describe something you could have used to help you get through that time but did not have.

3. What would be the absolute worst way to spend the rest of your life? Why?

4. What atrocities in the world make you sad and/or angry?

5. Dream big: What would you do with your life if money were no object?

STEPPING-STONE THREE
(A PLACE TO PREPARE THE WAY)

Dear Soul Shift Companion, one of the best ways to ease into the Practice of Offering Your Gift to the World is by traveling lightly. This means deciding from the start that you will not carry any unnecessary baggage, such as the seventy-pound "what-if" suitcase with the duct-taped handle and broken wheels.

For the life of me, I couldn't understand why I often got stuck while pursuing endeavors that felt so aligned with my heart and passions. Through a text exchange with a dear friend, I recognized a self-sabotaging habit and made an empowering declaration that has lightened my load ever since.

My friend had taken on a monumental task, one that she was deeply passionate about and had the skills to execute. Yet she was stuck by an overwhelming feeling of doubt. Her exact words were, "I feel incapable of the task before me, Rachel. What am I going to do?"

I didn't even have to think about my response. It poured from my fingertips, as if waiting for this moment to be realized. My response was this:

> My friend, I want to offer this thought—do not ask yourself to do more than you are being called to do. You need not ask if you are capable, how this project is going to turn

out, or how it's going to be received. Your job is to show up. Period. Your job is to keep putting one foot in front of the other. Your job is to focus solely on what you are being called to do TODAY, right now.

Do you know how I know this is the way through? Because I do this to myself! By trying to predict and plan what is unpredictable and unplannable, I often take on so much more than necessary! No wonder I get scared, nervous, and stuck!

So, do you know what I am going to do when I get weighed down by a What If? I am going to remind myself, "IT IS NOT YOUR JOB TO KNOW. Your job is to show up."

See where I am going here, my friend? By paring down that list to our most basic responsibilities, we eliminate the opportunity for fear and doubt to bog us down. So many of the things we worry about do not actually happen. So many of the things we try to plan and predict are not even relevant when we get a little further down the path and gain new perspective. So, let's not concern ourselves with things beyond our control. It's exhausting! Let's focus only on what our job is right now in this moment. One step at a time. My hand in yours.

I'll never forget my friend's response: "This advice is saving my life."
She then proceeded to tell me one specific thing she was going to do in that moment, and the next specific thing she was going to do after that. The two tasks were attainable and manageable, which meant she could breathe and actually enjoy the task her heart had led her to try.

Your Turn

Do you have a seventy-pound what-if suitcase with a duct-taped handle and broken wheels that comes out when you try to pursue something that delights your heart or gives you purpose? If so, take a minute to describe it.

In the tiny, easy-to-carry backpack below, draw three nurturing and supportive items you are going to take with you when you offer your gift to the world. They can be material or immaterial.

STEPPING-STONE FOUR
(A PLACE TO STEP OUT)

Dear Soul Shift Companion, now that you have experienced a bird's-eye view, learned to allow courage to navigate your way, and packed only the necessities, it is time to begin your Practice of Offering Your Gift to the World.

In this area of exploration, our habit shift is IN-COURAGING, which means using a combination of intuition and courage to contribute to the world in a way that matters to us. Why the combination? Because we do not get from the notion "offering my gift to the world will deplete me" to "following my heart's calling fulfills me" by accident. We get there through discernment, using our natural instinct and inherent courage to be selective about where we invest our gift.

Realistically, we know the requests of our time, energy, and talent aren't going to stop, and they certainly aren't going to magically align with our passions. Therefore, **we must align ourselves.** One of the most direct ways to do that is by focusing on whom or what you want to stand up for in your one, precious life.

When we narrow our focus to the people or causes that we want to positively impact, we become empowered to protect our energies in new ways. This most insightful truth came from an unforgettable passage in the book *Life Is a Verb* by author, educator, and expert on inclusion and meaning-making, Patti Digh. In it, she tells the story of a young Toni Morrison, at the time an aspiring author moonlighting as an editor at Random House publishers. One day Morrison made a to-do list.

"Faced with the long list," Digh writes, "she sat and looked at it for a long while, finally asking herself one question: 'What is it I must do or I shall die?' After answering that question, only two things on Toni Morrison's to-do list made the cut: 1) Be a mother to her children. 2) Write."

It was while reading this passage that I experienced the most powerful epiphany. I realized that *I* control what my daily to-do list looks like. And those day-to-day lists would eventually make up how I spent my life. By continuing to omit my heart's deepest delights and desires from the to-do list, I would never experience *my* true peace and joy.

What is it I must do or I shall die?

I decided to answer this powerful question. When it came right down to it, there were only two true desires for my time on earth:

1. Be a present and loving mother, partner, and human being.

2. Write words that make people feel seen and un-alone in the complexities of life.

I decided to call this my Life List.

Creating it enabled me to realize that when it really came down to it, there were only two vitally important goals—and they were worth pursuing and protecting with my very life. This discernment process spurred by my Life List was extremely helpful. By identifying these aspirations, it was much easier to see when I was choosing to engage in tasks that didn't support what was vitally important to me. From there, I was able to take steps to eliminate them from my schedule, using my practices of true self-worth and being my authentic self to stay strong and enforce boundaries.

Dear Soul Shift Companion, it's time to make your Life List.

To prepare a supportive mindset, I'd like you to either envision or hold a childhood photo as you read a message to a younger, and possibly more hopeful, version of yourself.

> Hello, young dreamer . . . Yes, I am speaking to you today, and I have a very important question to ask: What must you do before you leave this earth, precious one? No matter how outlandish the answer, write it. Say it. Scream it. Whisper it. Pray it. Believe it. A long time has passed since anyone really listened to you, but those years have not been wasted time. Oh no. Those experience-filled years have been preparing you for this moment when you, the Dreamer inside, is heard and believed. Now listen to these last five words very carefully: The world needs your gift. The world needs YOUR gift. Courage, please step forward.

In the heart below, please place your Life List. Don't overthink it . . . Just write whatever comes to mind when you ask yourself: *What must I do or I shall die?*

Study what you have written. Seal it into your mind because what you need to do now is simply *pay attention* . . . pay attention to the moments that make your heart full . . . moments that fill your eyes with tears . . . moments that make you say, "Hmm . . . I see an opportunity here that makes me feel a little excited and a little scared. Maybe, just maybe, it's time for COURAGE TO STEP FORWARD."

When one of these moments happens, draw a small heart on your living map in the back of the guide. Every time your heart sees a place where you have something to offer and you step forward, you are shedding your light of reclamation on your true path of peace and joy.

Commit to this vital practice by writing down the healing truth we uncovered today on a sticky note.

A PEACEFUL SPOT

(a Place to Let Things Sink In)

Stories:

**IN-COURAGING TO CAPTURE
THE POWER OF CONNECTION**

**IN-COURAGING TO CHAMPION
SOMEONE'S DREAM**

**IN-COURAGING TO
BRING EACH OTHER HOME**

In-Couraging to Capture the Power of Connection

One of the most uncomfortable aspects of public writing for me is sharing photos of myself on social media. Although it does not need to be a frequent occurrence, I feel it is important to periodically share the person behind the words. Whenever I do, I try to include a thoughtful caption.

One photo caption began like this: "This is me, Rachel, the human being behind this page. Some assume there's a team of people here, but it's just me . . ."

I quickly went back and removed the word *just*.

No one's presence is *just* anything, I reminded myself, and then I got lost in a memory . . .

Just before my eighth year of teaching special education, Scott and I moved to Florida. I accepted a job teaching a group of students who had exhausted all the special education resources the county had for students with severe behavioral issues.

At the end of the first day, I cried while driving home from work. The frustration and despair I felt that day only continued and intensified. For the first time in my teaching career, I felt completely inept.

What's the use? I remember asking myself after weeks of nonstop chaos and little progress. *Why should I keep trying?*

After one of the worst of the worst days, I scheduled a meeting with the associate principal of my school, Ms. Gensel. I'd decided I was going to ask to be transferred.

The next day, I sat across from Ms. Gensel prepared to describe the hopelessness and distress of that position. But before I spoke, she looked at me with genuine compassion. She said, "Thank you for showing up here every day. I can't know how hard it is, but I see you, and I thank you."

Ms. Gensel then gently folded her hands on her desk and leaned forward, indicating the floor was mine to express what was on my mind.

I proceeded to tell Ms. Gensel every heart-wrenching detail about the daunting task I'd been assigned. After she listened intently and helped me process some of the biggest obstacles, my heart revealed it was not time for me to move on; it was time for me to move a mountain by setting aside the proposed *curriculum* and focusing solely on *connection*. Right then and there, I decided connection would be the goal of each minute of each harrowing day. This shift in expectation, along with Ms. Gensel's support, breathed life into the situation, giving me a glimmer of hope.

Now, I'm not going to tell you that from that point on, everything miraculously turned around. But I *will* tell you that someone with the words "unable to form attachments" written in his thick student file began holding my hand when we walked to art class. Someone who tore apart the classroom on a regular basis started asking for time on the relaxation rug. Someone who couldn't be trusted with utensils made mashed potatoes for our class luncheon. Someone who'd hated school all twelve years of her young life hugged me and said, "I love our classroom."

And when that student said those words, I was grateful I hadn't stopped trying altogether; I just stopped trying what wasn't working and instead leaned on my basic instinct: *connection*.

Even in times of deep pain, distrust, chaos, and crisis, true connection has the power to bring healing and hope. That truth is in my fiber now as a parent, partner, friend, educator, and author. Natalie managed to capture it in one of the headshots I recently used as my social media profile picture.

I had the photo taken because Natalie asked me to take her senior photos for the yearbook.

"But don't you want a professional photographer to do that?" I'd asked, a bit surprised by the request.

"They will turn out much better if I'm with someone I feel comfortable with. And if you want, I can take your picture, too," she offered.

So, I put on my favorite blush pink dress, sat on some lovely steps, and watched Natalie position the camera like a true professional. I thought about what my talented friend Amy Paulson, who's taken almost all my author photos, would tell me to do with my hands, my body, my eyes.

"Think about what you want people to *feel* when they read your words," I could hear Amy say.

Un-alone.

That's the word I thought of when Natalie captured the most loving expression on my face.

More than anything, I wanted to express a heartfelt sentiment to the person on the other side of that photo: "You are not *just* anyone; you are someone whose presence matters, and I am so glad you are here."

Notes to Ponder

In this story, Rachel in-couraged by replacing curriculum with connection; in my life, I have in-couraged by replacing _____ with _____.

In-Couraging to Champion Someone's Dream

In 2018, I received an email from a complete stranger named Kelly explaining that she felt a connection to my work and wanted to offer support should I ever need anything. Although Kelly's career was in a completely different field, she explained that she loved to write, and she was good at writing, but hadn't exercised this gift in quite a while. Kelly expressed understanding for the undertaking of my work and offered to help by reviewing anything I'd like to have edited. I certainly could have just replied with a polite thank you and archived the correspondence, but something compelled me to reach out my hand instead.

I kept Kelly's message and reached out to her from time to time for small projects. Eventually, I was faced with a daunting task, writing a book on connection for parents of teens. When it was clear this would require intense writing and researching periods, I asked Kelly if she'd come through behind me after I wrote a chapter.

Not only did Kelly agree to help, but she added that I always seemed to show up at the right time, like when she wondered if she was giving this world everything she had to give . . . or when she craved a creative outlet . . . or when she needed strength and reassurance to navigate life after divorce. Although Kelly indicated I was helping her as much as she was helping me, I looked forward to the day I could properly thank her.

When I finished this massive project, which was my fourth book, part of me wanted to rush out and get Kelly a gift. But I knew this was not something to be rushed. When it was time, I'd know exactly how to thank her.

One day, the idea came to me, and I told my daughters I must go to a shop called Sugar Boo & Company. It was a locally owned shop filled with exquisite artifacts and vintage paper inscribed with the most uplifting words. I'd never seen so many gifts that encouraged people to dream their dreams.

Although it was a bit of a drive to the shop, I knew the moment I saw its unique sign that the effort had been worth it.

My daughter and I were only there for two minutes when we spotted my third book, *Only Love Today*, on the shelf. It took a minute for my brain to register what I was seeing because this wasn't a book shop; it was a gift shop! There were only a few books in stock, yet there was mine, nestled between a renowned poet and a novelist.

I stood there in awe remembering how I expressed my vision for the cover design of my first book. I'd said to my publisher, "You know the beautiful covers on the books at Anthropologie? That's what I am envisioning."

This wasn't Anthropologie, but it was close and maybe even better because this was a store that championed people's dreams.

After signing the store's stock of *Only Love Today*, I found the perfect gift for Kelly. It was an engraved leather journal with an elastic band to hold the abandoned dreams Kelly indicated were being unearthed through our partnership. I made my purchase and walked out of the store. I'd only walked a few steps when an internal nudge suggested I pause and take this moment in. I'd come to buy an "I-believe-in-your-dream" gift for someone who believed in mine, yet I walked away with three valuable guidelines for dreamers . . .

1. **Ask for help.** We are not meant to navigate life alone . . . and you just might bless someone by asking her to dust off her gift and join it with yours.

2. **Express gratitude for help.** There is no time limit, no *right* or *wrong* way to express gratitude, but when it feels like it's time to thank those who supported you, seize that feeling. As you prepare to offer thanks, you might just stumble upon a rare sight that will fuel your own heart.

3. **Expect miracles.** When you begin to pursue a dream and acknowledge that you can't do it alone, you may find yourself on your knees, opening your hands and your heart in ways you never have before. From that place of surrender, extraordinary things happen, and extraordinary people come into your life in order to bring that dream into the world.

I call those people Dream Companions. Kelly was mine, and I hope I can be hers now. This is how it works.

Notes to Ponder

I in-couraged my dream when I . . .

I in-couraged someone else's dream when I . . .

In-Couraging to Bring Each Other Home

One afternoon when my daughters and I were scheduled to volunteer at the cat shelter, I was feeling a bit anxious about an upcoming medical appointment. This uneasiness caused me to overreact when I noticed we were behind schedule. Although there is no set time that volunteers must report for their duties, I began shouting orders, saying we were going to be "late" to the shelter.

Appearing from her upstairs bedroom in her typical calm demeanor, Avery matter-of-factly stated, "Mom, there is no such thing as being late to help cats."

As my lips curved into a smile, my self-compassion kicked in and the internal pressure released. I was reminded that when we show up to do what our heart calls us to do, we are right on time . . . and we are gifted in ways we most need at that time.

That day, the gift came in the form of a soft-spoken gentleman. He had rescued an orange tabby named Carrot and cared for him until he found a trustworthy place that could find him a loving home.

When the man spoke, Carrot's sleeping head perked up.

"He knows your voice," I said in awe.

The man explained how he took food to the trailer park where Carrot was living and how he would wait each time to make sure Carrot ate the food. When it got extremely cold, the man couldn't leave him there, so he brought him home for a few nights. He then took him to the vet to get checked out and receive his shots.

Sensing how much the man loved this cat, I wondered why he couldn't keep him.

"I'm up to my limit—eight cats is the maximum," the man said, as if reading my mind.

And so there he was, doing his weekly visit to the cat shelter where Carrot was being given a chance to be adopted.

I enjoyed listening to the man talk to his furry friend. He knew what Carrot did and didn't like and who would make the perfect owner.

"You'll never play with these toys in your cage; you're more of a cuddler," the man said affectionately. "You never learned how to play because you were surviving. You'll make a wonderful companion for an elderly person who needs someone to snuggle with."

What the man didn't say was that he thought about Carrot all the time and couldn't rest until he had found his home. The man didn't have to say it—it came through clearly in the five words he kept repeating.

"Someone will come for you."

Those five words touched me so deeply that I couldn't seem to forget about them.

Several days after the visit, I found myself thinking about the man visiting the trailer park for many months and how he'd wait as long as was needed to ensure Carrot was nourished. I thought about how he sheltered Carrot from the cold and got him proper medical care.

What was in it for him? I kept wondering.

Some would say nothing. And perhaps I would have, too, had I not decided to forge a path to *my* true peace and purpose. Through this journey, I've learned that dedicating my time, energy, and focus to ensure a heart knows love, even if it's not mine to keep, is time well spent. That is how I want to spend my one, precious life.

"Someone will come for you," the man said over and over. I hoped he knew *he* was someone. Let us all be someone.

We really can't fully rest until we are all home.

P.S. One of the volunteers at the shelter was so inspired by the special bond between Carrot and his rescuer that she adopted Carrot herself. Carrot has been living his best cat life ever since.

Notes to Ponder

I felt in-couraged when I spent time and effort
nurturing _____, which I
knew was not mine to keep because . . .

INVITATION TO BLOOM

The Practice of Offering Your Gift to the World closes with an invitation rather than an assurance. This is a very special invitation, over a decade in the making, because before I could extend it, I had to experience it. Now it is your turn. Using the eight practices you have acquired through the Soul Shift journey and the healing discoveries you have made, you are capable of nurturing the joy and peace within yourself. This is an open-ended invitation, dear companion, to recognize, rediscover, and nourish your inherent gifts.

> I invite you to speak of remarkable things today—the things that make you feel alive . . . the things that bring you peace . . . the things that fill your eyes with tears . . . the things that feel like a "scary yes." Pay attention to those moments because they are telling you something deeply important about yourself. Even more, such moments offer clues that reveal the kind of offering you are born to make in this world.

> Your gift, calling, purpose—whatever you want to call it—is needed at this very moment. All you must do is step forward.

> You are ready.

> You are here.

YOU ARE
HOME

You've done it, weary human. You picked up this guide because something called you into the journey . . . but you didn't just accept the call, *you claimed it*, bravely, boldly, flawed and full of hope. Can I just tell you how proud I am of you? Of us? Together, we have traveled through eight groundbreaking areas of exploration. We have waded through muck and mud, battled the weeds, sought shelter, marked boundaries, released baggage, and found our footing. And because of these efforts, you are home!

Wait . . . this is home?

I can practically hear your bewilderment. You're thinking, *This? This can't be home; everything around me is still unpredictable, unfamiliar, chaotic, and uncertain.*

Remember, this journey has never been about overhauling your environment so you can thrive in *it*; it's always been about recognizing the ability to thrive is *inside you* . . . and learning how to access it, no matter what is going on around you.

On the Soul Shift journey, home is not a destination *out there*; it is an actualization *in here*, hand over heart. The moment you recognize *you* are home is the moment you are able to move through pain, uncertainty, and discomfort with your peace, purpose, and joy securely intact. I call these powerful moments Welcome Home Moments. Sometimes they occur during the experience; sometimes they become clear after the fact—but you can count on the awareness of your soul to nudge you when you navigate a situation, feeling, or memory using *your* truth as your guide. It just *feels* right, no external validation needed.

As you know by now, I believe concepts are best illustrated through examples. So, in that spirit, our final stop along this journey is my home, and the best way to show you around my home is through words. I am sharing them as they were written on the pages of a tiny notebook that lived inside my fanny pack until all its pages were filled. Forget about car keys and wallets and sunglasses; my fanny pack was made for pocket-sized notebooks and writing utensils to accompany me whenever I walk. In my most scribbled-in notebook, I captured the following observations, as they occurred, over the span of nine soul-shifting months. By the time I got to the fifth event, I connected the dots, and I recognized *Home* inside me.

Before you go your way and I go mine, I'd like to invite you in . . .

I AM HOME

I'm learning to walk differently through the world. I realize this when the physical therapist clicks her tongue after watching me "walk" across the room a few weeks after surgery.

She scribbles a note on her clipboard, then looks up and says, "To compensate for the pain, you've changed your gait. We'll need to strengthen parts of your feet, ankles, and calves that have become weak, basically teach you how to walk differently through the world."

Using an exercise band, I pull my foot in ways it does not want to go. New directions cause discomfort, but I don't want to limp through life in chronic pain, so I will keep stretching myself beyond my comfort zone.

I wish I'd addressed the pain before my body learned to compensate for it, but it's not too late to course-correct now. I am here. I am Home.

I'm learning to walk differently through the world. I realize this when my parents' retirement home finally opens to visitors after an extended shutdown due to COVID-19.

My parents and I encounter one of their dear friends in the hallway. The woman stops, looks directly in my eyes, and tearfully says, "Since I couldn't be with my family for such a long time, I really came to rely on your mom and dad. They have been good friends to me."

When the conversation ends, we begin to walk on. For the first time, I do not rush ahead. I wait on my dad, a polio survivor, whose gait forever changed when he contracted polio at age twelve. I think about him being isolated from his family for a year while he re-learned to walk.

I wish I'd known the impact of chronic pain and isolation sooner, but it's not too late to course-correct now. I am here. I am Home.

I'm learning to walk differently through the world. I realize this when a Soul Shift retreat participant approaches me after the morning workshop session to share her obstacles to healing as a Black woman. I listen as she describes her hurdles to education, health care, housing, income, safety, and justice.

After we talk, I adapt my plan for the afternoon session. I begin by emphasizing the importance of recognizing that we live in a world with systems that are advantageous to some and put others at a disadvantage. Therefore, our obstacles to joy, peace, and purpose are not the same. In hopes of bringing awareness to these discrepancies, which can then lead to actionable change, I offer the floor to those who would like to share their obstacles.

I sit down, and the woman I spoke with earlier comes forward. From the podium, her voice commands the room. She speaks as if she has prepared for this moment. What she shares is a memory of discrimination when she was in the first grade . . . then it is a glimpse of her fear when her son borrows the car . . . it is a declaration of worthiness from the boardroom . . . it is an expression of joy from her sister's porch . . . it is an invitation into the most important work of our lifetime.

Some members of the audience rise to their feet, accepting the invitation and committing to this work we must do together.

I wish I'd accepted my responsibility earlier in identifying and dismantling systemic obstacles to creating a more inclusive world, but it's not too late to course-correct now. I am here. I am Home.

I'm learning to walk differently through the world. I realize this when Avery asks me to go for a drive. I accept, focusing my attention on my breathing (not my out-of-tune voice) when we sing along to the radio.

This driving ritual began when her school shut down for many months during the global pandemic. For the first time in our lives, the goal of our excursions was not to go from point A to point B; the goal of the drive was to release and reset.

I made this connection while reading the book *Burnout*. In it, authors and sisters Amelia and Emily Nagoski explain how common it is for humans today to exist in a constant state of stress. The incomplete loops caused by ongoing cycles of stress build up, making it hard to sleep, focus, and be patient, and compromising our ability to manage the next stressful event. "To be 'well' is not to live in a state of perpetual safety and calm," the Nagoskis write, "but to move fluidly from a state of adversity, risk, adventure, or excitement, back to safety and calm, and out again. Stress is not bad for you; being stuck is bad for you."

This physical overload can lead to anxiety, depression, and stress-related illnesses. But with a few dedicated minutes each day, we can complete the stress response cycle with things like physical activity, slow, deep breaths, comfort from a loved one, and creative expression.

Given all this, it's no wonder our midday drives feel so restorative. No matter the weather, Avery extends her arms through the open window. For a moment, she's flying free from worry, transforming sadness into song, distress into breath.

As the Nagoskis explain, "Wellness happens when your body is a place of safety for you, even when your body is not necessarily in a safe place. You can be well, even during the times when you don't feel good."

I highlighted that paragraph in my copy of *Burnout*, but the permission it offers is forever ingrained in my mind. Existing in a constant state of stress is no longer something I have to accept as "just the way it is." With my newfound awareness, I am learning that I can restore my inner resources by engaging in activities that calm my nervous system. This allows me to manage the constant flow of life's challenges more effectively. Now I want the whole world to know that they, too, can learn to manage their reactions to stress and improve their overall well-being.

I wish I understood the damage of living in a constant state of stress sooner, but it's not too late to correct-course now. I am here. I am Home.

I'm learning to walk differently through the world. I realize this on the final day of my visit to my parents' retirement home. I venture out to the grounds, making sure to stop at the butterfly garden, as my dad suggested.

There are no butterflies. I feel concerned, so I wait.

That's when a wind chime above my head rings softly. The sound soothes me. I look up, and there is a tiny but determined ladybug crawling up the musical bar.

I count her dots . . .

One

Two

Three

Four

Five

When I was in elementary school, a ladybug landed on me during recess. My beloved teacher, Ms. Paluska, smiled and said something unforgettable: *"The presence of a ladybug means you are strong enough to handle any kind of change, Rachel."*

Her words didn't make sense to me then, but I loved my teacher, so I tucked them away for safekeeping.

Three decades, a million brave steps, five connective dots, and one long-awaited exhale later, they make complete sense. I believe it is no coincidence that the ladybug is here, the ideal mascot for the butterfly-less garden, a place where folks nearing the end of their days come to sit for a spell.

But today, she is here for me and for you . . .

A representative for childlike joy that we must never lose

A representative for small, determined steps that we must never underestimate

A representative for micro miracles that we must never fail to notice

A representative for healing shifts that we must not be afraid to make

The bright red mascot and I share a moment of solidarity, my dot to her dot. Then I shuffle away, mindful to use proper posture for my healing foot.

I'm learning to walk differently through the world.

It's not too late to course-correct.

I am here.

I am Home.

There is hope, hand over heart.

RESOURCES FOR THE JOURNEY

YOUR LIVING MAP

As noted in the introduction and throughout each area of exploration, the purpose of the living map is to document your Soul Shift discoveries, as they are happening, through color, symbols, and words. The living map below is a smaller reference version of the full-size map found on pages 242–243. You'll find the larger map has ample space to add your own personal elements and bring it to life. Watch as your Soul Shift journey steadily comes to life through your living map.

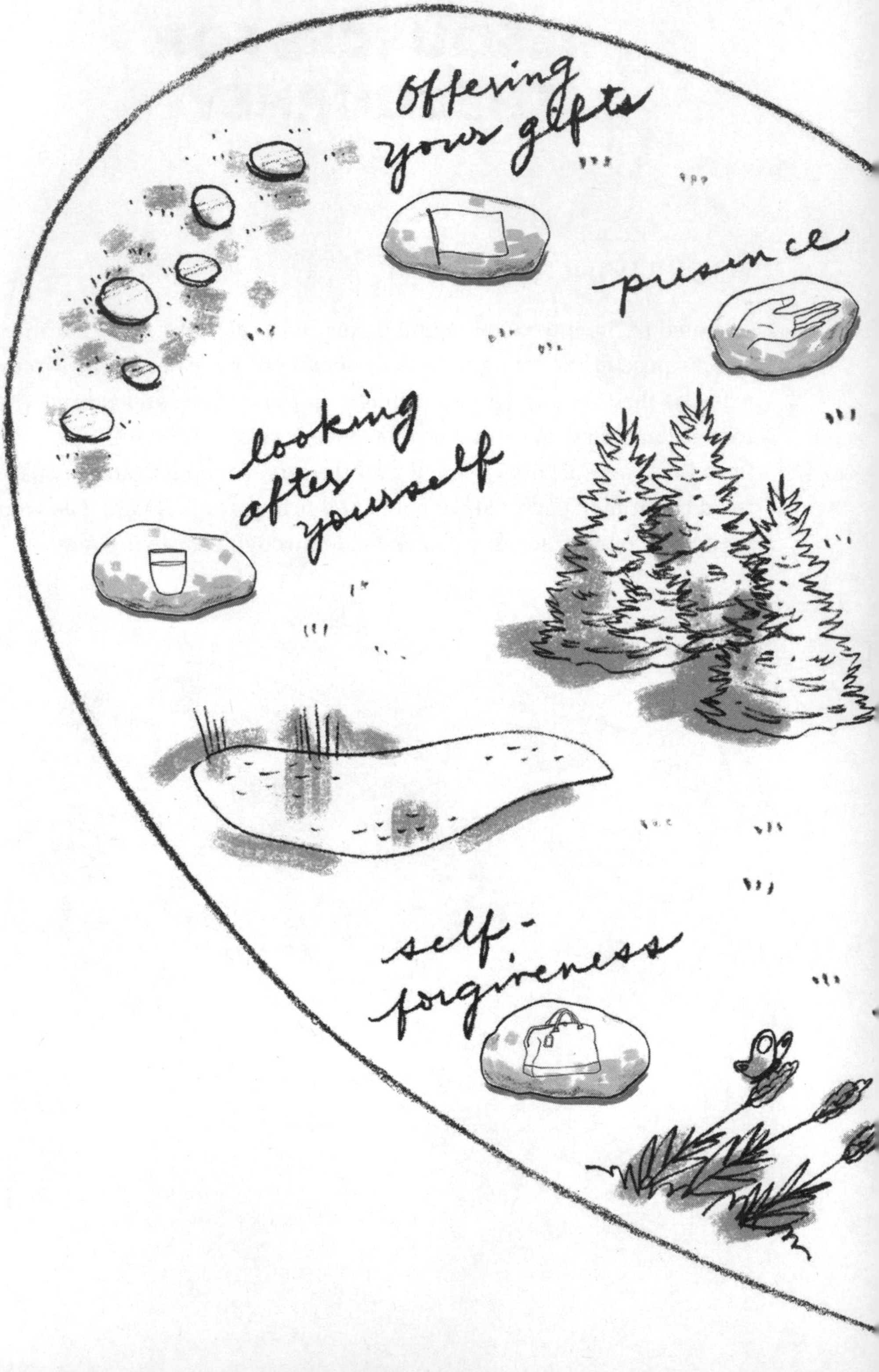
Offering your gifts
presence
looking after yourself
self-forgiveness

true self-worth

letting go
of perfection

being kind
to yourself

being your
authentic
self

MY SOUL SHIFT SOUNDTRACK

- "A Long December" by Counting Crows
- "All We Are" by Matt Nathanson
- "Another Way" by Kina Grannis
- "Back In My Body" by Maggie Rogers
- "Banks" by NEEDTOBREATHE
- "Be Here Now" by Ray LaMontagne
- "Beautiful Again" by JJ Heller
- "Best Part of Me" by Ed Sheeran
- "Collide" by Howie Day
- "Come Clean" by Tristan Prettyman
- "Cool Change" by Little River Band
- "Dear Me" by Nichole Nordeman
- "Healing" by Fletcher
- "Home" by Blue October
- "i believe" by Christina Perri
- "I Know the Way Home" by Andrew Galucki
- "I Remember Her" by Ingrid Michaelson
- "I Save Me" by Diane Warren and Maren Morris
- "Landslide" by Fleetwood Mac
- "Learning to Love Again" by Mat Kearney
- "Letting Go" by Ziggy Alberts
- "Little Voice" by Sara Bareilles
- "Look Up" by Joy Oladokun
- "Mess" by Noah Kahan
- "Oh Love" by Prateek Kuhad
- "Outnumbered" by Dermot Kennedy
- "Rainbow" by Kacey Musgraves
- "Same Old Things" by Black Match
- "This Is Why I Need You" by Jesse Ruben
- "Unpack Your Heart" by Phillip Phillips

Add your songs here:

-
-
-
-
-
-
-
-
-
-
-
-
-
-
-
-
-
-
-
-
-
-
-

YOU ARE NOT ALONE

Dear Soul Shift Companion, I applaud you for working through this guide and invite you to connect with other travelers who have pursued the quest to reclaim their joy through Soul Shift. On my website, handsfreemama.com, you can join my online community, discover my books, workshops, and audio series, and learn more about my mission to help people choose love as much as humanly possible.

Thank you for the gift of your presence.

My hand in yours,

ACKNOWLEDGMENTS

Unless you are one who flips to the back of a book and reads the acknowledgment section first (raises hand), then you probably know by now that I am a storyteller, not a bullet-point maker. Although I wrote this section of the book last and writer's fatigue was *very real*, you will not find a mere list of names here. What you *will* find is one last story, and if you are willing to walk beside me and listen, it may even feel like an acknowledgment to you.

This story begins with a life-changing gift I received when I was at the midpoint of writing this book.

The gift was a parking target Scott installed on the garage floor. The small, raised rubber stopper with reflective stripes let me know when it was time to push the brake so I didn't hit the wall.

Wait . . . you actually run into the garage wall? What kind of person are you?

It's okay if that's what you're thinking.

Yes, I am a Wall Bumper, have been for several decades. There are tiny Rachel dents in the garages of all five of the houses we've lived in over the past eighteen years.

The house where we currently live only has one dent, because now I have help.

It's okay to need help.

It's also okay if it takes time (even decades) to realize help is needed.

Because when you are ready to accept it, you often see that your problem isn't just about the obvious thing; it applies to other areas of your life, too.

It was while working on the last half of this book that I realized my wall-hitting tendencies expanded beyond the garage, particularly when it came to the book writing process. The publisher of my very first manuscript wanted it to go to press as quickly as possible, so they proposed a very tight submission deadline. Given that my middle name is Power Through, I eagerly agreed. By the time I realized the enormity of this endeavor, it was too late to turn back. So, when I encountered mental and physical walls throughout the writing process, I just forced myself to keep going, despite the toll it took.

This unhealthy yet efficient approach to meeting a publishing deadline set the precedent for my subsequent books, leaving me in a troubling state every single time.

Somewhere between Book #4 and Book #5, things changed. *I* changed.

I realized this when I found myself struggling to write the second half of this book. Given the circumstances of a global pandemic, chronic foot pain, and parenting teenagers, focusing for long periods of time was out of the question. When I found myself hitting a wall, I couldn't bring myself to forge ahead. It was as if my body recognized the danger of powering through and was no longer willing to sacrifice my health in the name of productivity.

Thus, I was faced with a dilemma: How will I meet my publisher's submission deadline?

Leave space.

That's what the little apparatus in the garage was helping me do, so I decided to apply it to the book writing process. On the days I could not string together coherent sentences, I used colorful construction paper, sticky notes, and vibrant markers to document ideas, organize thoughts, and plan out pages.

Spread across the family ping-pong table (often buried under the furry belly of Banjo), these colorful signs served as my stoppers. They said, "Don't hit a wall; plant a pause; give it space to flourish and grow."

For the first time in my eight-year authorship, I did not engage in self-sabotaging dialogue. Never once did I say, "I can't do this." What I said (a lot) was, "I can't do this today."

With one mere word, I was able to embrace a *trust-the-process* approach, which expanded the possibilities of what could be. I found that when the ability to focus *was* present, I was able to confidently pick up a colorful stack, fit the pieces together, and complete a small section of the book.

Slowly but surely, this creative and compassionate process helped me overcome big hurdles and make progress.

When I was 10,000 words shy of the required word count and two weeks away from the deadline, I received a text from Avery at school.

It read: "I know this is really short notice, but could we go see Grandma and Grandpa and visit the ocean during winter break?"

This human being, who was just starting to emerge from a long, dark, painful period, was inviting me to her place of peace.

For the first time in my work-before-play conditioned mind, I considered that looming deadline and knew exactly what to do. I placed a sticky note on my calendar that said, "BRB (be right back). There's something very important I need to tend to right now."

Leave space.

Exactly four days later, I found myself immersed in the butterfly garden of my parents' Florida retirement home.

While resting on the wooden bench surrounded by Cat Whiskers flowers, a recent conversation I had with my friend Shannon came back in full force. In a moment of complete and utter despair, I'd driven to the Target parking lot with no intention to go inside the store. I just needed a secluded place to process, scream, and cry.

Avery's stress response to the trauma of ongoing medical issues had fully come to light. Understanding the impact this adversity was having on her mental and physical health sent me reeling.

"I don't know what to do," I cried to Shannon.

"Yes, you do, Rachel. The answer is inside you, but you must make time and space to hear it."

Shannon spoke with such conviction that I believed what she was saying and promised I'd follow her guidance.

"Actually, I think I've already started," I realized, detecting a bit of hope in my voice. I explained how I'd stopped pushing myself to the point of exhaustion and even agreed to a last-minute beach trip with Avery, despite the looming book deadline.

My intuitive friend suddenly gasped with joy. "Rachel, I have chills all over my body. As you were speaking, I saw a garden of bright, colorful flowers, popping up, one by one . . . *pop pop pop pop*."

For days I carried Shannon's hopeful image with me, thinking it was a key for my child. But as I stared into the colorful sea of foliage before me, I knew my friend's vision was for me.

I'd only told a few people about my recurring fantasy to live a private life, working in a garden center, guiding customers to greenery that would enhance lives. My friend Diane's response to my admission was especially memorable. She said, "I can see it now . . . *Gardens by Rachel*."

At last, I could see it, too.

It was never a location, nor was it ever a job.

Gardens by Rachel was here, *inside me* all along, cultivated by a very special group of people who helped me arrive at this place of peace.

I see my garden refuge now, and the flowers all have names:

Kelly D. Diane C. Kerry F.

Shannon Sandra Lynn

Krystle Cindy Britt

Kaitlin Buzzy Kristie

Mary Maggie Carrie W.

Carrie B. Amy P. Caroline

Jaime Jennifer H. Kellie

Lizz Stacie Patti

Delpha Harry Rebecca

Natalie Avery Scott

_____

Dear Soul Shift Companion, if you have made it this far, thank you. You are a flower in my garden, too. Please add your name and celebrate the fact that you are part of this growing family who knows:

Life cannot be lived against the wall.

Self-reclamation cannot be rushed.

Works of heart cannot be forced.

When it comes to doing the things we are born to do, there is no timeline. The energy flows when it's supposed to flow; the ideas appear when we're open to receive them; the barriers weaken when we allow ourselves to breathe. The book you hold in your hands is not what I expected it to be; it is better because it has room for growth, grace, and goodness—things I did not plan for; they just came to be.

Leave space.

It is my way of life now, and will be for as long as my feet can carry me.

ABOUT THE AUTHOR

Rachel Macy Stafford is the *New York Times* bestselling author of *Hands Free Mama, Hands Free Life, Only Love Today,* and *Live Love Now*. Rachel is also a sought-after speaker, creator of her perennially popular online course, *Soul Shift*, and the narrator-guide of *Soul Shift Sessions*, her newest release. Rachel is a certified special education teacher whose personal strategies are universal invitations to embrace life with urgency and cultivate connection despite the distractions of our culture. Her blog and social media platform are a source of inspiration to millions. Rachel lives in Georgia with her beloved family. For more, visit handsfreemama.com.

ABOUT SOUNDS TRUE

Sounds True is a multimedia publisher whose mission is to inspire and support personal transformation and spiritual awakening. Founded in 1985 and located in Boulder, Colorado, we work with many of the leading spiritual teachers, thinkers, healers, and visionary artists of our time. We strive with every title to preserve the essential "living wisdom" of the author or artist. It is our goal to create products that not only provide information to a reader or listener but also embody the quality of a wisdom transmission.

For those seeking genuine transformation, Sounds True is your trusted partner. At SoundsTrue.com you will find a wealth of free resources to support your journey, including exclusive weekly audio interviews, free downloads, interactive learning tools, and other special savings on all our titles.

To learn more, please visit SoundsTrue.com/freegifts or call us toll-free at 800.333.9185.

sounds true
WAKING UP THE WORLD